LAW, CRIME AND LAW ENFORCEMENT

WHISTLEBLOWER PROTECTIONS

SELECT PROVISIONS AND ASSESSMENTS

LAW, CRIME AND LAW ENFORCEMENT

Additional books in this series can be found on Nova's website under the Series tab.

Additional e-books in this series can be found on Nova's website under the e-books tab.

LAWS AND LEGISLATION

Additional books in this series can be found on Nova's website under the Series tab.

Additional e-books in this series can be found on Nova's website under the e-books tab.

LAW, CRIME AND LAW ENFORCEMENT

WHISTLEBLOWER PROTECTIONS

SELECT PROVISIONS AND ASSESSMENTS

DARYL R. ARCELLONI
EDITOR

nova publishers
New York

For permission to use material from this book please contact us:
Telephone 631-231-7269; Fax 631-231-8175
Web Site: http://www.novapublishers.com

Additional color graphics may be available in the e-book version of this book.

Library of Congress Cataloging-in-Publication Data

ISBN: 978-1-62417-211-3

Published by Nova Science Publishers, Inc. † New York

CONTENTS

PREFACE

Legal protection for employees who report illegal misconduct by their employers have increased dramatically since the late 1970s when such protections were first adopted for federal employees in the Civil Service Reform Act of 1978. Since that time, with the enactment of the Whistleblower Protection Act of 1989, Congress has expanded such protections for federal employees. Congress has also established whistleblower protections for individuals in certain private-sector employment through the adoption of whistleblower provisions in at least 18 federal statutes. Among these statutes is the Sarbanes-Oxley Act, the FDA Food Safety Modernization Act, and the Dodd-Frank Wall Street Reform and Consumer Protection Act. This book provides an overview of key aspects of the 18 selected federal statutes applicable to individuals in certain private-sector industries. It focuses on the protections provided to employees who believe they have been subject to retaliation, rather than on how or where alleged misconduct should be disclosed.

Chapter 1 - Legal protections for employees who report illegal misconduct by their employers have increased dramatically since the late 1970s when such protections were first adopted for federal employees in the Civil Service Reform Act of 1978. Since that time, with the enactment of the Whistleblower Protection Act of 1989, Congress has expanded such protections for federal employees. Congress has also established whistleblower protections for individuals in certain private-sector employment through the adoption of whistleblower provisions in at least 18 federal statutes. Among these statutes is the Sarbanes-Oxley Act, the FDA Food Safety Modernization Act, and the Dodd-Frank Wall Street Reform and Consumer Protection Act (Dodd-Frank Act).

In general, claims for relief under the 18 federal statutes follow a similar pattern. Complaints are typically filed with the Secretary of Labor, and an investigation is conducted. Following the investigation, an order is issued by the Secretary, and a party aggrieved by the order is generally permitted to appeal the Secretary's order to a federal court. However, because 18 different statutes are involved in prescribing whistleblower protections, some notable differences exist. For example, under the Department of Defense Authorization Act of 1987, individuals employed by defense contractors who engage in whistleblowing activities file complaints with the Inspector General rather than the Secretary of Labor. Under some of the statutes, including the Commercial Motor Vehicle Safety Act and the Dodd-Frank Act, the Secretary's preliminary order will become a final order if no objections are filed within a prescribed time period.

This report provides an overview of key aspects of the 18 selected federal statutes applicable to individuals in certain private-sector industries. It focuses on the protections provided to employees who believe they have been subject to retaliation, rather than on how or where alleged misconduct should be disclosed. In addition, the report also includes an overview of the Whistleblower Protection Act. While state law may also provide whistleblower protections for employees, this report focuses only on the aforementioned federal statutory provisions.

Chapter 2 - This report discusses the federal statutory protections contained within the Whistleblower Protection Act (WPA) for federal employees who engage in "whistleblowing," that is, making a disclosure evidencing illegal or improper government activities. The protections of the WPA apply to most federal executive branch employees and become applicable where a "personnel action" is taken "because of" a "protected disclosure" made by a "covered employee." Generally, whistleblower protections may be raised within four forums or proceedings: (1) employee appeals to the Merit Systems Protection Board of an agency's adverse action against an employee, known as "Chapter 77" appeals; (2) actions instituted by the Office of Special Counsel; (3) individually maintained rights of action before the Merit Systems Protection Board (known as an individual right of action, or IRA); and (4) grievances brought by the employee under negotiated grievance procedures.

On March 9, 2007, the House Committee on Oversight and Government Reform reported H.R. 985 (110th Cong.) H.Rept. 110-42, the Whistleblower Protection Enhancement Act of 2007, which would amend the WPA by providing protections for certain national security, government contractor, and science-based agency whistleblowers, and by enhancing the existing whistleblower protections for all federal employees.

Chapter 3 - Whistleblowers help guard the federal government against waste, fraud, and abuse. The Military Whistleblower Protection Act provides servicemembers with a means to seek relief from reprisals and to hold subjects accountable. GAO was asked to determine the extent to which the Department of Defense (DOD) has (1) satisfied statutory timeliness requirements for processing military whistleblower reprisal cases, (2) established and implemented oversight mechanisms for its process, and (3) taken corrective action in cases where the DOD Inspector General (DODIG) substantiated reprisal claims. GAO also analyzed case characteristics. GAO examined laws, regulations, and guidance documents; interviewed officials from DODIG, service IGs, service Boards for the Correction of Military Records (BCMRs), and the Office of the Undersecretary of Defense for Personnel and Readiness; and collected and analyzed case data. GAO also conducted a detailed file review using a representative sample of cases closed between January 1, 2009 and March 31, 2011.

Chapter 4 - The Tax Relief and Health Care Act of 2006 expanded the Internal Revenue Service's (IRS) whistleblower program, increasing rewards for submitting information on others' tax underpayments to up to 30 percent of collected proceeds. The expanded program targets tax underpayments over $2 million and could reduce the gap between taxes owed and taxes paid. IRS's Whistleblower Office has received over 1,300 submissions qualifying for this new program since 2007.

GAO was asked to assess (1) how IRS manages the expanded program, (2) how IRS communicates with whistleblowers and the public, and (3) any lessons from IRS's or other government whistleblower programs that could improve IRS's expanded whistleblower program. GAO analyzed IRS documents and data and interviewed IRS officials, whistleblower attorneys, and federal and state whistleblower program officials.

In: Whistleblower Protections
Editor: Daryl R. Arcelloni

ISBN: 978-1-62417-211-3

Chapter 1

WHISTLEBLOWER PROTECTIONS UNDER FEDERAL LAW: AN OVERVIEW*

Jon O. Shimabukuro and L. Paige Whitaker

SUMMARY

Legal protections for employees who report illegal misconduct by their employers have increased dramatically since the late 1970s when such protections were first adopted for federal employees in the Civil Service Reform Act of 1978. Since that time, with the enactment of the Whistleblower Protection Act of 1989, Congress has expanded such protections for federal employees. Congress has also established whistleblower protections for individuals in certain private-sector employment through the adoption of whistleblower provisions in at least 18 federal statutes. Among these statutes is the Sarbanes-Oxley Act, the FDA Food Safety Modernization Act, and the Dodd-Frank Wall Street Reform and Consumer Protection Act (Dodd-Frank Act).

In general, claims for relief under the 18 federal statutes follow a similar pattern. Complaints are typically filed with the Secretary of Labor, and an investigation is conducted. Following the investigation, an order is issued by the Secretary, and a party aggrieved by the order is generally permitted to appeal the Secretary's order to a federal court. However, because 18 different statutes are involved in prescribing

* This is an edited, reformatted and augmented version of a Congressional Research Service publication, CRS Report for Congress R42727, from www.crs.gov, prepared for Members and Committees of Congress, dated September 13, 2012.

whistleblower protections, some notable differences exist. For example, under the Department of Defense Authorization Act of 1987, individuals employed by defense contractors who engage in whistleblowing activities file complaints with the Inspector General rather than the Secretary of Labor. Under some of the statutes, including the Commercial Motor Vehicle Safety Act and the Dodd-Frank Act, the Secretary's preliminary order will become a final order if no objections are filed within a prescribed time period.

This report provides an overview of key aspects of the 18 selected federal statutes applicable to individuals in certain private-sector industries. It focuses on the protections provided to employees who believe they have been subject to retaliation, rather than on how or where alleged misconduct should be disclosed. In addition, the report also includes an overview of the Whistleblower Protection Act. While state law may also provide whistleblower protections for employees, this report focuses only on the aforementioned federal statutory provisions.

INTRODUCTION

Legal protections for employees who report illegal misconduct by their employers have increased dramatically since the late 1970s when such protections were first adopted for federal employees in the Civil Service Reform Act of 1978. Since that time, with the enactment of the Whistleblower Protection Act of 1989, as amended, Congress has expanded such protections for federal employees. Congress has also established whistleblower protections for individuals in certain private-sector employment through the adoption of whistleblower provisions in at least 18 other industry-specific federal statutes. For example, in 2002, Congress passed the Sarbanes-Oxley Act (SOX) in response to corporate scandals that occurred in the late 1990s and early 2000s. SOX established new civil protections for employees who report concerns about alleged fraud upon shareholders. More recently, Congress passed the FDA Food Safety Modernization Act (FDA Modernization Act), which prohibits entities engaged in food manufacturing, processing, and related activities from discharging or otherwise discriminating against an employee for providing information related to any violation or act that the employee reasonably believes to be a violation of the Federal Food, Drug, and Cosmetic Act.[1]

This report provides an overview of whistleblower provisions in 19 selected federal statutes. While state law may also provide whistleblower protections for employees, this report focuses on relevant federal statutory provisions. The report does not discuss the qui tam and whistleblower provisions of the False Claims Act that permit private citizens with knowledge of fraud against the federal government to sue on its behalf and receive a portion of the recovered proceeds.

CLEAN AIR ACT (CAA)

The CAA prohibits an employer from discharging or otherwise discriminating against any employee with respect to his or her compensation, terms, conditions, or privileges of employment because the employee (1) commenced or is about to commence a proceeding under the CAA or a proceeding for the administration or enforcement of any requirement imposed by the CAA; (2) testified or is about to testify in any such proceeding; or (3) assisted or participated or is about to assist or participate in any manner in such a proceeding.[2] Any employee who believes that he or she has been discharged or otherwise discriminated against in violation of the CAA may, within 30 days after such violation occurs, file a complaint with the Secretary of Labor. Upon receipt of the complaint, the Secretary will conduct an investigation and within 30 days of the receipt of such complaint, shall notify the complainant and the alleged violator with the results of the investigation. Within 90 days of receipt of the complaint, the Secretary shall issue an order either providing relief or denying the complaint. If the Secretary determines that a violation has occurred, the Secretary will order the person who committed such violation to (1) take affirmative action to abate the violation, and (2) reinstate the complainant to his or her former position with compensation, including back pay, terms, conditions, and privileges of employment. The Secretary may order the payment of compensatory damages to the complainant. If an order is issued, at the request of the complainant, the Secretary will assess against the person against whom the order is issued a sum equal to the aggregate amount of all costs and expenses, including attorneys' and expert witness fees, reasonably incurred by the complainant in bringing the complaint.[3]

Any person adversely affected or aggrieved by an order issued under the CAA's whistleblower provisions may obtain review of the order in the U.S. court of appeals for the circuit in which the violation allegedly occurred. The petition for review must be filed within 60 days from the issuance of the Secretary's order, and the commencement of proceedings shall not, unless ordered by the court, operate as a stay of the Secretary's order.

> The Secretary may file a civil action in the U.S. district court in which the violation occurred when a person has failed to comply with an order.

An order by the Secretary is not subject to judicial review in any criminal or other civil proceeding. When a person has failed to comply with an order, the Secretary may file a civil action in the U.S. district court in which the violation occurred and the district courts shall have jurisdiction to grant all appropriate relief, including injunctive relief, as well as compensatory and exemplary damages.[4] Any person on whose behalf an order was issued may commence a civil action against the person to whom such order was issued to require compliance, and the appropriate U.S. district court shall have jurisdiction, without regard to the amount in controversy or citizenship of the parties. In issuing any final order, the court may award costs of litigation, including reasonable attorney and expert witness fees, to any party whenever the court determines it is appropriate.[5]

Commercial Motor Vehicle Safety Act (CMVSA)

The CMVSA prohibits employers from discharging, disciplining, or discriminating against an employee regarding pay, terms, or privileges of employment because the employee filed a complaint or instituted a proceeding related to a violation of a commercial motor vehicle safety regulation, standard, or order, or has testified or will testify in such proceeding. Additionally, any employee who refuses to operate a vehicle because the operation violates a regulation, standard, or order related to commercial motor vehicle safety or health, or has a reasonable apprehension of serious injury because of the vehicle's unsafe condition, is likewise protected from such retaliatory action.[6]

An employee alleging discharge, discipline, or discrimination in violation of the CMVSA may file a complaint with the Secretary of Labor within 180 days after the alleged violation occurred. Within 60 days of receiving the complaint, the Secretary will conduct an investigation, decide whether the complaint has merit, and notify the complainant and the person alleged to have committed the violation of the findings. If the Secretary determines that it is reasonable to believe that the violation occurred, the Secretary will include in the findings a preliminary order for relief. Within 30 days of receiving notice of the Secretary's findings, the complainant and person alleged to have committed the violation may file objections to the findings or preliminary order and request a hearing on the record, although the filing of objections does not stay a reinstatement ordered in the preliminary order. If a hearing is not requested within 30 days, the preliminary order is final and not subject to judicial review. A hearing shall be conducted expeditiously, and not later than 120 days after the end of the hearing, the Secretary will issue a final order. Before the final order is issued, the proceeding may be ended by settlement agreement by the Secretary, the complainant, and the person alleged to have committed the violation. If the Secretary determines that a violation of this provision occurred, he or she can order the person alleged to have committed the violation to (1) take affirmative action to abate the violation; (2) reinstate the complainant to the former position with the same pay and terms and privileges of employment; and (3) pay compensatory damages, including back pay. Upon request by the complainant, the Secretary may assess against the person against whom the order is issued the costs, including attorneys' fees, reasonably incurred by the complainant in bringing the complaint.[7]

Within 60 days after an order is issued, a person adversely affected may file a petition for review in the U.S. court of appeals for the circuit in which the violation occurred or the person resided on the date of the violation. The review will be heard and decided expeditiously and an order is not subject to judicial review in a criminal or other civil proceeding. If a person fails to comply with an order issued under this provision, the Secretary will bring a civil action to enforce the order in the U.S. district court for the judicial district in which the violation occurred.[8]

Comprehensive Environmental Response Compensation and Liability Act of 1980 (CERCLA)

CERCLA, also known as the "Superfund" Act, prohibits an employer from firing or in any other way discriminating against, or causing to be fired or discriminated against, any employee because that employee provided information to a state or the federal government; filed, instituted, or caused to be filed or instituted any proceeding under the statute; or has testified or will testify in a proceeding resulting from the administration or enforcement of the statute.[9] Any employee who believes that he or she has been terminated or otherwise discriminated against by any person in violation of CERCLA's whistleblower provisions may, within 30 days, apply to the Secretary of Labor for a review of the termination or alleged discrimination. Upon receipt of such application, the Secretary will institute an investigation and upon receiving the investigation report, make findings of fact. If the Secretary finds that a violation occurred, she will issue a decision, incorporating an order, requiring the party committing the violation to take such affirmative action to abate the violation as the Secretary deems appropriate, including reinstatement to the former position with compensation. If she finds no violation, the Secretary will issue an order denying the application. An order issued by the Secretary is subject to judicial review.[10] When an order is issued under this provision, at the request of the applicant, a sum equal to the aggregate amount of all costs and expenses, including attorneys' fees, will be assessed against the person committing such violation.[11]

> Defense contractor employees who engage in whistleblowing activities file complaints with the Inspector General (IG) rather than the Secretary of Labor.

DEPARTMENT OF DEFENSE AUTHORIZATION ACT OF 1987

The Department of Defense Authorization Act of 1987 prohibits defense contractors from discharging, demoting, or otherwise discriminating against an employee as a reprisal for disclosing to a Member of Congress, an authorized official of an agency, or the Department of Justice information relating to a substantial violation of law related to a contract, including the competition for or negotiation of a contract.[12] Any person who believes that he or she has been subject to a prohibited reprisal may submit a complaint to the Inspector General (IG), who is required to investigate the complaint unless the IG determines that the complaint is frivolous. Upon completion of the investigation, the IG will submit a report of the findings of the investigation to the individual, relevant contractor, and the head of the agency.[13] If the agency head determines that a contractor has subjected a person to a prohibited reprisal, the agency head may take one or more of the following actions: (1) order the contractor to abate the reprisal; (2) order the contractor to reinstate the person to the position that the person held before the reprisal, together with compensation, including back pay, employment benefits, and other applicable terms and conditions of employment; (3) order the contractor to pay the complainant an amount equal to the aggregate amount of all costs and expenses, including attorneys' and expert witnesses' fees, that were reasonably incurred by the complainant.[14] If a person fails to comply with such an order, the agency head will file an action for enforcement in the U.S. district court for the district in which the reprisal occurred. The court may grant appropriate relief, including injunctive relief, as well as compensatory and exemplary damages.[15] Within 60 days after the order is issued, any person adversely affected or aggrieved by such an order may obtain review in the U.S. court of appeals for a circuit in which the reprisal occurred.[16]

DODD-FRANK WALL STREET REFORM AND CONSUMER PROTECTION ACT (DODD-FRANK ACT)

The Dodd-Frank Act established several new whistleblower protections for individuals employed in the financial services industry. Section 748 of the Dodd-Frank Act, for example, amended the Commodity Exchange Act (CEA) to prohibit employers from discharging or otherwise discriminating against an individual for providing information related to a violation of the CEA to the Commodity Futures Trading Commission (CFTC) or for assisting in any investigation or judicial or administrative action of the CFTC based upon or related to such information. An individual who alleges a termination or other discrimination in violation of the CEA provisions may bring an action in the appropriate district court of the United States. If the individual is a federal employee, he or she must bring the action in accordance with Section 1221 of Title 5, U.S. Code.[17] An individual who prevails in a whistleblower action will be awarded reinstatement, back pay with interest, and compensation for any special damages sustained as result of the discharge or discrimination, including litigation costs and reasonable attorney's fees.

> An individual who prevails in an action under Section 21F will be awarded two times the amount of back pay otherwise owed.

Section 922 of the Dodd-Frank Act amended the Securities Exchange Act of 1934 to add a new Section 21F that prohibits employers from discharging or otherwise discriminating against an individual for (1) providing information related to a violation of the securities laws to the Securities and Exchange Commission (SEC); (2) initiating, testifying in, or assisting in any investigation or judicial or administrative action of the SEC based upon or related to such information;or (3) making disclosures that are required by SOX, the Securities Exchange Act of 1934, or any other law subject to the

SEC's jurisdiction. An individual who alleges a termination or other discrimination in violation of these provisions may bring an action in the appropriate district court of the United States. An individual who prevails in a whistleblower action under Section 21F will be awarded reinstatement, two times the amount of back pay otherwise owed to the individual, with interest, and compensation for litigation costs, expert witness fees, and reasonable expenses.

Section 1057 of the Dodd-Frank Act prohibits employers engaged in providing consumer financial products or services, and employers that provide a material service in connection with the provision of such products or services, from terminating or in any other way discriminating against a covered employee because the employee has (1) provided, caused to be provided, or is about to provide or cause to be provided, information relating to a violation of Title X of the Dodd-Frank Act or any other provision of law that is subject to the jurisdiction of the Bureau of Consumer Financial Protection (Bureau) to the employer, the Bureau, or a state, local, or federal government authority or law enforcement agency; (2) testified or will testify in any proceeding resulting from the administration or enforcement of Title X of the Dodd-Frank Act or any other provision of law that is subject to the jurisdiction of the Bureau; (3) filed, instituted, or caused to be filed or instituted any proceeding under any federal consumer financial law; or (4) objected to or refused to participate in any activity that the employee reasonably believed to be in violation of any law subject to the jurisdiction of, or enforceable by, the Bureau.[18]

An employee who believes that he or she has been discharged or otherwise discriminated against in violation of the Section 1057 whistleblower provisions may file a complaint with the Secretary of Labor within 180 days of the alleged violation. Within 60 days after receiving the complaint, the Secretary will initiate an investigation and determine whether there is reasonable cause to believe that the complaint has merit. The Secretary will notify the complainant and the person alleged to have committed the violation of her determination in writing. If the Secretary concludes that there is reasonable cause to believe that a violation has occurred, she will also issue a preliminary order that provides relief. Either party may file objections to the Secretary's findings or order and request a hearing within 30 days after receiving her notification. If a hearing is not requested in the 30-day period, the preliminary order shall be deemed a final order that is not subject to judicial review.[19]

If a hearing is conducted, the Secretary is required to issue a final order providing relief or denying the complaint within 120 days after the date of the hearing's conclusion. If the Secretary determines that a violation has occurred, she may order the person who committed the violation to take affirmative action to abate the violation, order the reinstatement of the complainant to his or her former position with compensation, including back pay, and order the payment of compensatory damages. At the request of the complainant, the Secretary will also assess against the person who committed the violation a sum equal to the aggregate amount of all legal costs and expenses reasonably incurred. Any person adversely affected or aggrieved by a final order may seek review of the order in the U.S. court of appeals for the circuit in which the violation allegedly occurred or the circuit in which the complainant resided on the date of such violation. If the Secretary fails to issue a timely final order, the complainant may seek *de novo* review in the appropriate district court of the United States having jurisdiction.

Energy Reorganization Act of 1974 (ERA)

The ERA prohibits employers from discharging or otherwise discriminating against any employee who (1) notified his or her employer of an alleged violation of the ERA or the Atomic Energy Act of 1954 (AEA); (2) refused to engage in any unlawful practice under the ERA or AEA, if the employee identified the alleged illegality to the employer; (3) testified before Congress or at any federal or state proceeding regarding any provision of the ERA or AEA; (4) commenced a proceeding under the ERA or AEA; (5) testified or is about to testify in any such proceeding; or (6) assisted or participated or is about to assist or participate in a proceeding to carry out the purposes of the ERA or AEA.[20] Any employee who believes that he or she has been discharged or otherwise discriminated against in violation of the ERA's whistleblower provisions may, within 180 days after such violation occurs, file a complaint with the Secretary of Labor alleging such discharge or discrimination. Upon receipt of a complaint, the Secretary will complete an investigation within 30 days. Within 90 days of receiving the complaint, the Secretary will, unless the proceeding is terminated due to a settlement, issue an order either providing relief or denying the complaint. Upon the conclusion of a public hearing and the issuance of a recommended decision that the complaint has merit, the Secretary will issue a preliminary order providing relief, but may not order compensatory damages pending a final order.

> The Secretary will dismiss a complaint and not conduct an investigation unless the complainant has made a prima facie showing that the protected action was a contributing factor in the alleged unfavorable personnel action.

If the Secretary determines that a violation has occurred, she will order the person who committed such violation to (1) take affirmative action to abate the violation, and (2) reinstate the complainant to his former position together with compensation, including back pay, terms, conditions, and privileges of his or her employment. The Secretary may order the person who committed the violation to provide compensatory damages to the complainant. If an order is issued, the Secretary, at the request of the complainant, will assess a sum equal to the aggregate amount of all costs and expenses, including attorneys' and expert witness fees, reasonably incurred by the complainant. The Secretary will dismiss a complaint and not conduct an investigation unless the complainant has made a prima facie showing that the protected action by the employee was a contributing factor in the unfavorable personnel action alleged in the complaint. Notwithstanding a finding by the Secretary that the complainant has made the required prima facie showing, no investigation shall be conducted if the employer demonstrates, by clear and convincing evidence, that it would have taken the same unfavorable personnel action in the absence of such behavior. Relief may not be ordered if the employer demonstrates by clear and convincing evidence that it would have taken the same unfavorable personnel action in the absence of such behavior.[21]

Any person adversely affected by an order issued under the ERA's whistleblower provisions may obtain review of the order in the U.S. court of appeals for the circuit in which the violation allegedly occurred. A petition for review must be filed within 60 days of the issuance of the Secretary's order. Review shall conform to chapter 7 of Title 5, U.S. Code, and the commencement of proceedings under this provision shall not, unless ordered by the court, operate as a stay of the Secretary's order.

An order by the Secretary shall not be subject to judicial review in any criminal or other civil proceeding. Whenever a person fails to comply with an order issued under this provision, the Secretary may file a civil action in the U.S. district court for the district in which the violation occurred. In actions brought under this provision, the district courts shall have jurisdiction to grant all appropriate relief, including injunctive relief and compensatory and exemplary damages. Any person on whose behalf an order was issued may commence a civil action against the person to whom such order was issued to require compliance with such order; the appropriate U.S. district court shall have jurisdiction, without regard to the amount in controversy or citizenship of the parties; and in issuing any final order under this subsection, the court may award costs of litigation, including reasonable attorney and expert witness fees.[22]

FAIR LABOR STANDARDS ACT OF 1938 (FLSA)

The FLSA prohibits employers from discharging or otherwise discriminating against an employee because such employee filed a complaint or instituted any proceeding under the statute, testified or is about to testify in any such proceeding, or served or is about to serve on an industry committee.[23] Employers who willfully violate the FLSA's anti-retaliation provisions may be fined up to $10,000 and imprisoned up to six months. Employers who retaliate against employees in violation of this provision shall be liable for legal and equitable relief, including, without limitation, reinstatement, the payment of lost wages, and an additional equal amount as liquidated damages. An action may be maintained against any employer, including a public agency, in any federal or state court of competent jurisdiction by any one or more employees. The court shall, in addition to any judgment awarded, allow reasonable attorneys' fees to be paid to the plaintiff, as well as the costs of the action. An employee loses his or her right to file a complaint under this provision once the Secretary of Labor files a complaint against the employer.[24]

> Willful violations of the FLSA's anti-retaliation provisions could result in fines up to $10,000 and imprisonment up to six months.

FDA FOOD SAFETY MODERNIZATION ACT (FDA MODERNIZATION ACT)

The FDA Modernization Act amended the Federal Food, Drug, and Cosmetic Act to prohibit an entity engaged in the manufacture, processing, packing, transporting, distribution, reception, holding, or importation of food from discharging or otherwise discriminating against an employee with respect to the individual's compensation, terms, conditions, or privileges of employment because the employee (1) provided, caused to be provided, or is about to provide or cause to be provided information relating to a violation of the Federal Food, Drug, and Cosmetic Act to the employer, the federal government, or the attorney general of a state; (2) testified or is about to testify in a proceeding concerning the violation; (3) assisted or participated or is about to assist or participate in a proceeding concerning the violation; or (4) objected to, or refused to participate in any activity that the employee believed to be in violation of the Federal Food, Drug, and Cosmetic Act.[25]

An individual who believes that he or she has been discharged or otherwise discriminated against in violation of the relevant whistleblower provisions may file a complaint with the Secretary of Labor within 180 days after the date on which the violation occurs.[26] Within 60 days of receiving the complaint, the Secretary will initiate an investigation and determine whether there is reasonable cause to believe that the complaint has merit. If the Secretary determines that reasonable cause exists, she will accompany her findings with a preliminary order that requires the person who committed the violation to take affirmative action to abate the violation, to reinstate the complainant to his or her former position with compensation, and to provide compensatory damages. The person alleged to have committed the violation or the complainant may file objections to the findings or the preliminary order and request a hearing. A final order must be issued by the Secretary within 120 days after the date of the hearing's conclusion. If the Secretary fails to issue a timely final decision, the complainant may seek *de novo* review in the appropriate district court of the United States with jurisdiction.

FEDERAL MINE SAFETY AND HEALTH ACT (FMSHA)

The FMSHA prohibits an employer from discharging an employee or applicant for employment because the individual (1) filed or made a complaint under or related to the FMSHA; (2) is the subject of medical evaluations and potential transfer; (3) instituted or testified in any proceeding under or related to the FMSHA; or (4) exercised any statutory right afforded by the FMSHA.[27] Employees and applicants who believe that they have been discharged, interfered with, or otherwise discriminated against in violation of this prohibition may file a complaint with the Secretary of Labor within 60 days after the alleged violation. Upon receipt of the complaint, the Secretary will forward a copy to the respondent and within 15 days of receiving the complaint, the Secretary will institute an investigation as she deems appropriate. If the Secretary determines that the complaint was not brought frivolously, the Federal Mine Safety and Health Review Commission will order the immediate reinstatement of the miner pending a final order. If the Secretary determines that the FMSHA's whistleblower provisions have been violated, she will immediately file a complaint with the Commission, with service upon the alleged violator and miner, proposing an order granting appropriate relief. The Commission shall afford an opportunity for a hearing and shall issue an order, affirming, modifying, or vacating the Secretary's proposed order, or directing other appropriate relief. The Commission retains the authority to require a person committing a violation to abate the violation as the Commission deems appropriate, including the rehiring or reinstatement of the miner to his or her former position with back pay and interest.[28]

> If the Secretary determines that the complaint was not brought frivolously, the Federal Mine Safety and Health Review Commission will order the immediate reinstatement of the miner pending final order.

Within 90 days of receiving a complaint, the Secretary will notify the miner about whether a violation occurred. If the Secretary determines that the FMSHA's whistleblower provisions were violated, the complainant shall have the right to file an action in his or her own behalf before the Commission. The Commission shall afford an opportunity for a hearing and shall issue an order, granting such relief as it deems appropriate. Whenever an order is issued sustaining a complainant's charges, a sum equal to the aggregate amount of all costs and expenses, including attorneys' fees, will be assessed against the person who committed the violation. Any person adversely affected by such an order may obtain review in any U.S. court of appeals for the circuit in which the violation is alleged to have occurred or in the U.S. Court of Appeals for the D.C. Circuit.[29]

FEDERAL WATER POLLUTION CONTROL ACT OF 1972 (FWPCA)

The FWPCA prohibits an employer from firing or otherwise discriminating against an employee, or causing such firing or discrimination, because the employee has filed, instituted, or caused to be filed or instituted any proceeding under the FWPCA, or has testified or is about to testify in any proceeding resulting from the administration or enforcement of the FWPCA.[30]

Any employee who believes that he or she has been fired or discriminated against in violation of this provision may, within 30 days after such alleged violation occurs, apply to the Secretary of Labor for a review. Upon receipt of such application, the Secretary will institute an investigation as he or she deems appropriate. Upon receiving the report of such investigation, the Secretary will make findings of fact; if she finds that such violation did occur, the Secretary will issue a decision, incorporating an order and findings, requiring the party committing such violation to take such affirmative action to abate the violation, including the rehiring or reinstatement of the employee with compensation. If the Secretary finds that there was no such violation, she will issue an order denying the application; such order shall be subject to judicial review in the same manner as orders and decisions are subject to judicial review under 33 U.S.C. §§ 1251 *et seq.* Whenever an order is issued, at the request of the applicant, a sum equal to the aggregate amount of all costs and expenses, including attorneys' fees, determined to have been reasonably incurred by the applicant, will be assessed against the person committing the violation.

LONGSHORE AND HARBOR WORKERS' COMPENSATION ACT (LHWCA)

The LHWCA prohibits an employer from discharging or otherwise discriminating against an employee who claims or attempts to claim compensation from the employer, or testifies or is about to testify against the employer in a proceeding under the statute. Any employer who violates this provision will be liable for a penalty of not less than $1,000 nor more than $5,000. If such penalties are not paid, they may be recovered in a civil action brought in the appropriate U.S. district court.

> If the employee ceases to be qualified to perform the duties of employment, the employee will not be restored to his or her position and will not be compensated for any wage loss.

Any employee that is discriminated against under the statute's whistleblower provisions shall be restored to his or her employment and shall be compensated for any loss of wages arising from the discrimination, provided that if the employee ceases to be qualified to perform the duties of employment, he or she shall not be entitled to such restoration and compensation. The employer and not his insurance carrier shall be liable for such penalties and payments, and any provision in an insurance policy undertaking to relieve the employer from the liability for such penalties and payments shall be void.[31]

Migrant and Seasonal Agricultural Worker Protection Act (MSAWPA)

The MSAWPA prohibits employers from intimidating, threatening, restraining, coercing, blacklisting, discharging, or in any manner discriminating against any migrant or seasonal agricultural worker because such worker has, with just cause, filed a complaint or instituted, or caused to be instituted, any proceeding under the statute's anti-retaliation provisions. Additionally, any employee who has testified or is about to testify in any such proceeding or justifiably exercises any right or protection afforded by MSAWPA is protected from retaliatory action.[32] An employee who believes, with just cause, that he or she has been discriminated against in violation of the relevant provisions may file a complaint with the Secretary of Labor within 180 days of the violation. As she deems appropriate, the Secretary will institute an investigation and, upon determining that a violation has occurred, will bring an action in any appropriate U.S. district court. In any such action, the U.S. district court will have jurisdiction, for cause shown, to restrain the violation and order all appropriate relief, including reinstatement with back pay or damages.[33]

Occupational Safety and Health Act of 1970 (OSH Act)

The OSH Act prohibits employers from discharging or in any manner discriminating against an employee because such employee filed a complaint or instituted or caused to be instituted a proceeding under the OSH Act, or is about to testify in any such proceeding. Additionally, any employee who has testified or is about to testify in any such proceeding or exercises any right or protection afforded by the OSH Act is protected from retaliatory action. An employee who believes that he or she has been discharged or otherwise discriminated against in violation of the OSH Act may file a complaint with the Secretary of Labor alleging such discrimination within 30 days. Upon receipt of such complaint, the Secretary will institute an investigation as she deems appropriate. If the Secretary determines that a violation has occurred, she will bring an action in any appropriate U.S. district court. The U.S. district court shall have jurisdiction, for cause shown, to restrain the violation and order all appropriate relief including reinstatement with back pay.[34]

SAFE DRINKING WATER ACT (SDWA)

The SDWA prohibits employers from firing, or in any other way discriminating against, or causing to be fired or discriminated against, any employee because such employee filed, instituted, or caused to be filed or instituted any proceeding under the SDWA or has testified or is about to testify in any proceeding resulting from the administration or enforcement of the SDWA. Any employee who believes that he or she has been fired or otherwise discriminated against in violation of the SDWA may, within 30 days after such alleged violation occurs, apply to the Secretary of Labor for a review. Upon receipt of such application, the Secretary will initiate an investigation as she deems appropriate. Upon receiving the report of such investigation, the Secretary will make findings of fact; if she finds that such violation did occur, the Secretary will issue a decision, incorporating an order and findings, requiring the party committing such violation to take such affirmative action to abate the violation, including, the rehiring or reinstatement of the employee with compensation. If the Secretary finds that there was no such violation, she will issue an order denying the application; such order is subject to judicial review in the same manner as orders and decisions are subject to judicial review under 42 U.S.C. §§ 6901 *et seq.* Whenever an order is issued, at the request of the applicant, a sum equal to the aggregate amount of all costs and expenses, including attorneys' fees, determined to have been reasonably incurred by the applicant, shall be assessed against the person who committed the violation.[35]

Any employee or employer adversely affected or aggrieved by an order may obtain review of the order in the U.S. court of appeals for the circuit in which the violation allegedly occurred. Within 60 days of the issuance of the order, the petition for review must be filed and review shall conform to 5 U.S.C.§§ 701 *et seq.* An order of the Secretary shall not be subject to judicial review in any criminal or other civil proceeding. Whenever a person has failed to comply with an order, the Secretary will file a civil action in the U.S. district court for the district in which the violation occurred. In actions brought under the SDWA's whistleblower provisions, the district courts shall have jurisdiction to grant all appropriate relief, including injunctive relief and compensatory and exemplary damages.[36]

SARBANES-OXLEY ACT OF 2002 (SOX)

SOX prohibits publicly traded companies, including any subsidiaries or affiliates whose financial information is included in the consolidated financial statements of such companies, and nationally recognized statistical rating organizations from discharging, demoting, suspending, threatening, harassing, or in any other manner discriminating against an employee because such employee provided information, caused information to be provided, otherwise assisted in an investigation or filed, testified, or participated in a proceeding regarding any conduct that the employee reasonably believes is a violation of SOX, any SEC rule or regulation, or any federal statute relating to fraud against shareholders, when the information or assistance is provided to a federal regulatory or law enforcement agency, any Member or committee of Congress, or a person with supervisory authority over the employee or investigative authority for the employer, regarding any violation of 18 U.S.C. §§ 1341 (mail fraud), 1343 (wire fraud), 1344 (bank fraud), 1348 (securities fraud against shareholders), or any SEC rule or regulation, or of any federal law regarding fraud against shareholders.[37] Any employee who alleges such wrongful discharge or other discrimination may file a complaint with the Secretary of Labor, using procedures set forth in 49 U.S.C. § 42121(b). In the absence of delay resulting from an employee's bad faith, the employee may seek *de novo* review in the appropriate U.S. district court, if the Secretary of Labor does not issue a final decision within 180 days. An action must be commenced within 180 days after the date on which the violation occurs.[38]

A prevailing employee may be awarded all relief necessary to make the individual whole, including reinstatement with pre-discrimination seniority status, back pay with interest, and compensation for any special damages incurred as a result of the discrimination, including litigation costs, expert witness fees, and reasonable attorneys fees, and to leave the employee with all rights, privileges or remedies under federal or state law or any collective bargaining agreement.[39]

An employee prevailing in a whistleblower action may be awarded all relief necessary to make the individual whole.

SOLID WASTE DISPOSAL ACT (SWDA)

The SWDA prohibits employers from firing, or in any other way discriminating against, or causing to be fired or discriminated against, any employee because such employee filed, instituted, or caused to be filed or instituted any proceeding under the SWDA, or has testified or is about to testify in any proceeding resulting from the administration or enforcement of the SWDA.[40] Any employee who believes that he or she has been fired or otherwise discriminated against in violation of the SWDA's whistleblower provisions may, within 30 days after such alleged violation occurs, apply to the Secretary of Labor for a review. Upon receipt of such application, the Secretary will institute an investigation as she deems appropriate. Following the receipt of the investigation report, the Secretary will make findings of fact; if she finds that a violation did occur, the Secretary will issue a decision, incorporating an order and findings, requiring the party committing such violation to take such affirmative action to abate the violation, including the rehiring or reinstatement of the employee with compensation. If the Secretary finds no violation, she will issue an order denying the application; such order shall be subject to judicial review in the same manner as orders and decisions are subject to judicial review under 42 U.S.C. §§ 6901 et seq.[41] Whenever an order is issued, at the request of the applicant, a sum equal to the aggregate amount of all costs and expenses, including attorneys' fees, to have been reasonably incurred by the applicant, will be assessed against the person who committed the violation.[42]

SURFACE MINING CONTROL AND RECLAMATION ACT (SMCRA)

The SMCRA prohibits employers from discharging or in any other way discriminating against or causing to be fired or discriminated against any employee because such employee has filed, instituted, or caused to be filed or instituted any proceeding under this provision. Additionally, any employee who has testified or is about to testify in any such proceedings is protected from such retaliatory action.[43] An employee who believes that he or she has been fired or otherwise discriminated against in violation of the SMCRA's whistleblower provisions may, within 30 days, apply to the Secretary of Labor for a review of such firing or alleged discrimination. Upon receipt of such complaint, the Secretary will initiate an investigation as she deems appropriate. If the Secretary determines that a violation occurred, she will issue a decision incorporating the findings of fact and an order requiring the party committing the violation to take such affirmative action to abate the violation as the Secretary deems appropriate, including the rehiring or reinstatement of the employee with compensation. If the Secretary finds that no violation occurred, she shall issue a finding. Orders issued by the Secretary shall be subject to judicial review in the same manner as other orders and decisions of the Secretary are subject to judicial review under the SMCRA.[44] Whenever an order is issued to abate a violation, at the request of the applicant, a sum equal to the aggregate amount of all costs and expenses, including attorney's fees, determined to have been reasonably incurred by the applicant in connection with the institution and prosecution of such proceedings, shall be assessed against the person who committed the violation.[45]

TOXIC SUBSTANCES CONTROL ACT (TSCA)

The TSCA prohibits employers from discharging or otherwise discriminating against any employee with respect to compensation, terms, conditions, or privileges of employment because the employee has (1) commenced, caused to be commenced, or is about to commence or cause to be commenced a proceeding under the TSCA; (2) testified or is about to testify in any such proceeding; or (3) assisted or participated or is about to assist or participate in such a proceeding or in any other action to carry out the purposes of the TSCA.[46] Any employee who believes that he or she has been discharged or otherwise discriminated against by any person in violation of the TSCA's whistleblower provisions may, within 30 days after such alleged violation occurs, file a complaint with the Secretary of Labor. Upon receipt of such a complaint, the Secretary will conduct an investigation and within 30 days of the receipt of such complaint, the Secretary will complete such investigation. Within 90 days of receiving the complaint, the Secretary will, unless the proceeding is terminated due to a settlement, issue an order either providing relief or denying the complaint. The Secretary may not enter into a settlement terminating a proceeding on a complaint without the participation and consent of the complainant. If the Secretary determines that a violation of this provision has occurred, the Secretary will (1) order the person who committed such violation to take affirmative action to abate the violation, (2) order such person to reinstate the complainant to the complainant's former position together with the compensation, including backpay, terms, conditions, and privileges of the complainant's employment, (3) order compensatory damages, and (4) where appropriate, order exemplary damages. Whenever an order is issued, at the request of the applicant, a sum equal to the aggregate amount of all costs and expenses, including attorneys' fees will be assessed against the person who committed the violation.[47] Any employee or employer adversely affected or aggrieved by an order may obtain review of the order in the U.S. court of appeals for the circuit in which the violation allegedly occurred. The petition for review must be filed within 60 days of the issuance of the order. Such review must conform to 5 U.S.C.§§ 701 *et seq*. Whenever a person has failed to comply with an order, the Secretary will file a civil action in the U.S. district court for the district in which the violation was found to occur. In actions brought under the TSCA's whistleblower provisions, the district courts shall have jurisdiction to grant all appropriate relief, including injunctive relief and compensatory and exemplary damages.[48]

WHISTLEBLOWER PROTECTION ACT (WPA)

The WPA[49] generally provides protections for federal employees who make disclosures evidencing illegal or improper government activities. In order to trigger the protections of the WPA, a case must contain the following elements: a "personnel action" that was taken because of a "protected disclosure" made by a "covered employee."

Covered Employees

Although anyone may disclose whistleblowing information for referral to the appropriate agency, an investigation and report from the head of that agency is required only if the information is received from a "covered employee." In addition, with few exceptions, prohibited personnel practices apply only to covered employees. Therefore, as a threshold matter, it is important to note which federal employees are statutorily covered.

To trigger protections under the WPA, a case must contain the following elements, as defined under the act:

- A personnel action
- A protected disclosure
- A covered employee

Generally, current employees, former employees, or applicants for employment to positions in the executive branch of government and the Government Printing Office, in both the competitive and the excepted service, as well as positions in the Senior Executive Service, are considered covered employees.[50] However, those positions that are excepted from the competitive service because of their "confidential, policy-determining, policy-making, or policy-advocating character,"[51] and any positions exempted by the President based on a determination that it is necessary and warranted by conditions of good administration,[52] are not protected by the whistleblower statute.

Moreover, the statute does not apply to federal workers employed by the U.S. Postal Service or the Postal Rate Commission,[53] the Government Accountability Office, the Federal Bureau of Investigation,[54] the Central Intelligence Agency, the Defense Intelligence Agency, the National Geospatial-Intelligence Agency, the National Security Agency, and any other executive entity that the President determines primarily conducts foreign intelligence or counter-intelligence activities.[55] Agency heads are required to inform their employees of these protections.[56]

Protected Disclosures

Any disclosure of information that a covered employee reasonably believes evidences "a violation of any law, rule, or regulation" or evidences "gross mismanagement, a gross waste of funds, an abuse of authority, or a substantial and specific danger to public health or safety" is protected on the condition that the disclosure is not prohibited by law nor required to be kept secret by Executive Order in the interest of national defense or foreign affairs.[57] Moreover, any disclosure made to the Special Counsel or to the Inspector General of an agency or another employee designated by the head of the agency to receive such disclosures, which the employee reasonably believes evidences "a violation of any law, rule, or regulation," or evidences "gross mismanagement, a gross waste of funds, an abuse of authority, or a substantial and specific danger to public health or safety" is also protected.[58] In addition, the WPA expressly provides that the statute is not to be interpreted as "authoriz[ing] the withholding of information from the Congress or the taking of any personnel action against an employee who discloses information to the Congress."[59]

Personnel Actions

The WPA protects employees from reprisals in the form of an agency taking or failing to take a "personnel action." This encompasses a broad range of actions by an agency having a negative or adverse impact on the employee. The statute specifically defines the term "personnel action" to include 11 areas of agency activity:

> (i) an appointment; (ii) a promotion; (iii) an action under chapter 75 of this title or other disciplinary or corrective action; (iv) a detail, transfer, or reassignment; (v) a reinstatement; (vi) a restoration; (vii) a reemployment; (viii) a performance evaluation under chapter 43 of this title; (ix) a decision concerning pay, benefits, or awards, or concerning education or training if the education or training may reasonably be expected to lead to an appointment, promotion, performance evaluation, or other action described in this subparagraph; (x) a decision to order psychiatric testing or examination; and (xi) any other significant change in duties, responsibilities, or working conditions.[60]

The WPA also expressly protects employees from prohibited personnel practices taken because they engaged in activities that are often related to whistleblowing, including exercising any appeal, complaint, or grievance right granted by law, rule, or regulation, testifying for others or lawfully assisting others in any such appeal, complaint, or grievance right; cooperating with or disclosing information to an agency Inspector General or the Special Counsel; or for refusing to obey an order that would be in violation of law.[61]

Forums Where Whistleblower Protections May Be Raised

Under the WPA, there are three general forums or proceedings where whistleblower protections may be raised: (A) in employee appeals to the Merit Systems Protection Board (MSPB) of an agency's adverse action against the employee under chapter 77;[62] (B) in actions instituted by the Office of Special Counsel (OSC);[63] and (C) in individual rights of action.[64] Beyond the statutory provisions of the WPA, the defense or claim of reprisal for whistleblowing might also be raised in a grievance proceeding initiated by an employee pursuant to a grievance procedure that was negotiated through collective bargaining between the employee's agency and the employee union.[65] An aggrieved employee affected by a prohibited personnel action is precluded from choosing more than one of the above remedies.[66]

Under the WPA, whistleblower protections may be raised in three general forums or proceedings:

1. Employee appeals to the MSPB under chapter 77
2. Actions instituted by the Office of Special Counsel
3. Individual rights of action

Employee Appeals to the MSPB Under Chapter 77

The MSPB is authorized to hear and rule on appeals by employees regarding agency actions affecting the employee and that are appealable to the Board by law, rule, or regulation.[67] Types of agency actions against employees that are appealable to the MSPB and in which an employee may raise the defense of reprisal for whistleblowing as a prohibited personnel practice include adverse actions against the employee for "such cause as will promote the efficiency of the service" (generally referred to as conduct-based adverse actions),[68] and performance-based adverse actions against employees for "unacceptable performance."[69] In such appeals, an agency's decision and action will not be upheld if the employee "shows that the decision was based on any prohibited personnel practice described in section 2302(b) of this title."[70] If the MSPB finds that an employee or applicant for employment has prevailed in an appeal, the employee or applicant may be provided with interim relief, pending the outcome of any petition of review.[71] Moreover, the Special Counsel may not intervene in an appeal under chapter 77 without the consent of the individual bringing the appeal.[72]

Actions by the Office of Special Counsel (OSC)

The WPA established the OSC as an agency independent from the MSPB.[73] Its primary responsibilities, however, have remained essentially the same as set forth in its statutory predecessor, the Civil Service Reform Act (CSRA). With the goal of protecting employees, former employees, and applicants for employment from prohibited personnel practices, the OSC has the duty to receive allegations of prohibited personnel practices and to investigate such allegations,[74] as well as to conduct an investigation of possible prohibited personnel practices on its own initiative, absent any allegation.[75]

The Special Counsel has several avenues available through which to pursue allegations, complaints, and evidences of reprisals for whistleblowing activities, including (1) requiring agency investigations and agency reports concerning actions the agency is planning to take to rectify those matters referred;[76] (2) seeking an order for "corrective action" by the agency before the MSPB;[77] (3) seeking "disciplinary action" against officers and employees who have committed prohibited personnel practices;[78] (4) intervening in any proceedings before the MSPB, except that in cases where an individual has brought an individual right of action (IRA) under Section 1221 or an appeal to the MSPB under chapter 77, the OSC must first obtain the individual's consent;[79] and (5) seeking a stay from the MSPB for any personnel action pending an investigation.[80]

Investigations[81]

Within 240 days of receipt of a complaint, the OSC must make a determination as to whether there are reasonable grounds to believe that a prohibited personnel practice has occurred, exists, or is to be taken.[82] If a positive determination is made and the information was sent to the Special Counsel by an employee, former employee, applicant for employment, or an employee who obtained the information acting within the scope of employment,[83] the Special Counsel must transmit the information to the appropriate agency head and require that the agency head conduct an investigation and submit a written report.[84] The identity of the complaining employee may not be disclosed without such individual's consent, unless the Special Counsel determines that disclosure is necessary to avoid imminent danger to health and safety or an imminent criminal violation.[85] The Special Counsel then reviews the reports as to their completeness and the reasonableness of the findings[86] and submits the reports to Congress, the President, the Comptroller General,[87] and the complainant.[88]

If the Special Counsel does not make a positive determination, however, he or she may only transmit the information to the agency head with the consent of the individual.[89] Further, if the Special Counsel receives the information from some source other than the ones described above, he or she *may* transmit the information to the appropriate agency head who shall inform the Special Counsel of any action taken.[90] In any case where the subject of the whistleblowing disclosure evidences a criminal violation, however, all information is referred to the Attorney General and no report is transmitted to the complainant.[91]

At least every 60 days throughout its investigation, the OSC must give notice of the status of the investigation to the individual who brought the allegation.[92] In addition, no later than 10 days before the termination of an investigation, a written status report including the proposed findings and legal conclusions must be made to the individual who made the allegation of wrongdoing.[93]

Corrective Actions

If in any investigation the Special Counsel determines that there are "reasonable grounds to believe" a prohibited personnel practice exists or has occurred, the Special Counsel must report findings and recommendations, and may include recommendations for corrective action, to the MSPB, the agency involved, the Office of Personnel Management (OPM) and, optionally, to the President.[94] If the agency does not act to correct the prohibited personnel practice, the Special Counsel may petition the MSPB for corrective action.[95] The MSPB, before rendering its decision, is required to provide an opportunity for oral or written comments by the Special Counsel, the agency involved and the OPM, and for written comments by any individual who alleges to be the victim of the prohibited personnel practices.[96]

The WPA made it easier for a complainant to prove retaliation for whistleblowing in a corrective action before the MSPB. The Special Counsel need only prove by a preponderance of the evidence that the disclosure was a "contributing factor" in the personnel action, instead of a "significant factor."[97] In addition, once the MSPB renders a final order or decision of corrective action, complainants have the right to judicial review in the U.S. Court of Appeals for the Federal Circuit.[98]

In what is probably the most significant change from its statutory predecessor, the CSRA, the WPA increased the standard by which an agency must prove its affirmative defense that it would have taken the personnel action even if the employee had not engaged in protected conduct. Once the complainant's *prima facie* case of reprisal has been established by showing that the whistleblowing was a contributing factor in the personnel action, the government is required to demonstrate by "clear and convincing evidence" that it would have taken the same personnel action even in the absence of such disclosure.[99] Under the CSRA, the government's standard of proof was a "preponderance of the evidence." "Clear and convincing evidence," although a lesser standard than the criminal standard of "beyond a reasonable doubt," is greater than "preponderance of the evidence."

Disciplinary Actions

Proceedings for disciplinary action against an officer or employee who commits a prohibited personnel practice may be instituted by the Special Counsel by filing a written complaint with the MSPB.[100] After proceedings before the MSPB or an administrative law judge,[101] if violations are found, the MSPB may impose any of various disciplinary actions, including removal, reduction in grade, debarment from federal employment for a period not to exceed five years, suspension, reprimand, or an assessment of civil fines up to $1,000.[102] In addition, the agency involved may be held responsible for reasonable attorney's fees.[103] In the case of presidentially appointed and Senate confirmed employees in "confidential, policy-making, policy-determining, or policy-advocating" positions, the complaint and the statement of facts, along with any response from the employee, are to be presented to the President for disposition in lieu of the presentation to the Board.[104]

Intervention

As a matter of right, the Special Counsel may intervene or otherwise participate in any proceedings before the MSPB, except that in cases where an individual has brought an individual right of action (IRA) under Section 1221, discussed below, or an appeal to the MSPB under chapter 77, the OSC must first obtain the individual's consent.[105]

Stays

Upon application by the OSC, a member of the MSPB may stay or postpone, for 45 days, pending an investigation, a personnel action that the Special Counsel has reasonable grounds to believe constitutes a prohibited personnel practice, unless the member determines that a stay would not be appropriate under the circumstances.[106] If no MSPB member acts within three days of the OSC application, the stay becomes effective.[107] After the employing agency has had an opportunity to comment on the appropriateness of extending a stay, the MSPB may extend it.[108] A stay may be terminated by the MSPB at any time, except that a stay may not be terminated by the MSPB on its own motion or on the motion of an agency, unless notice and opportunity for oral or written comments are first provided to the Special Counsel and the individual on whose behalf the stay was ordered; or on a motion of the Special Counsel, unless notice and opportunity for oral or written comments are first provided to the individual on whose behalf the stay was ordered.[109]

Individual Right of Action (IRA)

The WPA provides that an employee, former employee, or applicant for employment has the independent right to seek review of whistleblower reprisal cases by the MSPB no more than 60 days after notification is provided to such employee that the investigation was closed or 120 days after filing a complaint with the OSC.[110] As a result of the IRA statutory provisions, a greater number of employees, including probationers, temporaries, and those in the excepted service, have a method of appeal to the MSPB for whistleblower reprisals that was not previously available under the CSRA.[111] In addition, retired employees are not barred from instituting this type of appeal.[112]

If the employee is the prevailing party before the MSPB, based on the finding of a prohibited personnel practice, or if the employee is the prevailing party in an appeal to the MSPB, regardless of the basis of the decision, the WPA provides several remedies. These may include placing the individual, as nearly as possible, in the position the individual would have been in had the prohibited personnel practice not occurred, awarding back pay and related benefits, recompensing medical costs incurred, travel expenses, or any other reasonable and foreseeable consequential charges.[113] In all cases, corrective action includes awarding attorneys' fees.[114] The MSPB findings can be based on circumstantial evidence.[115] Moreover, the Special Counsel may not intervene in an individual right of action without the consent of the individual bringing the appeal.[116]

End Notes

[1] P.L. 111-353, 124 Stat. 3885.
[2] 42 U.S.C. § 7622(a).
[3] 42 U.S.C. § 7622(b).
[4] 42 U.S.C. § 7622(d).
[5] 42 U.S.C. § 7622(e).

[6] 49 U.S.C. § 31105(a).
[7] 49 U.S.C. § 31105(b).
[8] 49 U.S.C. § 31105(c), (d).
[9] 42 U.S.C. § 9610(a).
[10] 42 U.S.C. § 9610(b).
[11] 42 U.S.C. § 9610(c).
[12] 10 U.S.C. § 2409(a).
[13] 10 U.S.C. § 2409(b).
[14] 10 U.S.C. § 2409(c)(1).
[15] 10 U.S.C. § 2409(c)(2).
[16] 10 U.S.C. § 2409(c)(3).
[17] See P.L. 111-203, § 748, 124 Stat. 1376, 1739 (2010).
[18] P.L. 111-203, § 1057(a), 124 Stat. 1376, 2031 (2010). The term "covered employee" is defined to include "any individual performing tasks related to the offering or provision of a consumer financial product or service."
[19] P.L. 111-203, § 1057(c)(2)(C), 124 Stat. 1376, 2032-33 (2010).
[20] 42 U.S.C. § 5851(b).
[21] Id.
[22] 42 U.S.C. § 5851(c).
[23] 29 U.S.C. § 215(a)(3).
[24] 29 U.S.C. § 216(b).
[25] 21 U.S.C. § 1012(a).
[26] 21 U.S.C. § 1012(b)(1).
[27] 30 U.S.C. § 815(c)(1).
[28] 30 U.S.C. § 815(c)(2).
[29] 30 U.S.C. § 816.
[30] 33 U.S.C. § 1367(a).
[31] 33 U.S.C. § 948a.
[32] 29 U.S.C. § 1855(a).
[33] 29 U.S.C. § 1855(b).
[34] 29 U.S.C. § 660(c).
[35] 42 U.S.C. § 300j-9(i)(1),(2).
[36] 42 U.S.C. § 300j-9(i)(3),(4).
[37] 18 U.S.C. § 1514A(a).
[38] 18 U.S.C. § 1514A(b)(2)(D).
[39] 18 U.S.C. § 1514A(c), (d).
[40] 42 U.S.C. § 6971(a).
[41] 42 U.S.C. § 6971(b).
[42] 42 U.S.C. § 6971(c).
[43] 30 U.S.C. § 1293(a).
[44] 30 U.S.C. § 1293(b).
[45] 30 U.S.C. §1293(c).
[46] 15 U.S.C. § 2622(a).
[47] 15 U.S.C. § 2622(b).
[48] 15 U.S.C. § 2622(c),(d).
[49] P.L. 101-12, 103 Stat. 16; P.L. 103-424, 108 Stat. 4361 (codified, as amended, in various sections of Title 5 U.S.C.).
[50] 5 U.S.C. § 2302(a)(2)(B).

[51] 5 U.S.C. § 2302(a)(2)(B)(i).
[52] 5 U.S.C. § 2302(a)(2)(B)(ii).
[53] 5 U.S.C. § 2105(e).
[54] Another provision of federal law prohibits personnel practices in the FBI as a reprisal for a disclosure of information to the Attorney General or his or her designee that the employee reasonably believes evidences "(1) a violation of any law, rule, or regulation, or (2) mismanagement, a gross waste of funds, an abuse of authority, or a substantial and specific danger to public health or safety." 5 U.S.C. § 2303(a)(1),(2).
[55] 5 U.S.C. § 2302(a)(2)(C).
[56] 5 U.S.C. § 2302(c).
[57] 5 U.S.C. § 2302(b)(8)(A).
[58] 5 U.S.C. § 2302(b)(8)(B).
[59] 5 U.S.C. § 2302(b). Based on the legislative history regarding this provision of the WPA, it appears that Congress sought to protect its right to receive even "confidential" information from federal employees, without employee fear of reprisals: The provision is intended to make clear that by placing limitations on the kinds of information any employee may publicly disclose without suffering reprisal, there is not intent to limit the information an employee may provide to Congress or to authorize reprisal against an employee for providing information to Congress. For example, 18 U.S.C. 1905 prohibits public disclosure of information involving trade secrets. That statute does not apply to transmittal of such information by an agency to Congress. Section 2302(b)(8) of this act would not protect an employee against reprisal for public disclosure of such statutorily protected information, but it is not to be inferred that an employee is similarly un-protected if such disclosure is made to the appropriate unit of the Congress. Neither title I nor any other provision of the act should be construed as limiting in any way the rights of employees to communicate with or testify before Congress. H.Rept. 95-1717 (Conference Report) (1978), reprinted in 1978 U.S. CODE CONG. & ADMIN. NEWS 2861. See also 5 U.S.C. § 7211, providing that an employee is guaranteed the right to freely petition or furnish information to Congress, a Member of Congress, a committee, or a Member thereof.
[60] 5 U.S.C. § 2302(a)(2)(A).
[61] 5 U.S.C. § 2302(b)(9).
[62] 5 U.S.C. § 7701.
[63] 5 U.S.C. §§ 1211-1215.
[64] 5 U.S.C. § 1221.
[65] 5 U.S.C. § 7121.
[66] 5 U.S.C. § 7121(g)(2).
[67] 5 U.S.C. § 7701, 5 U.S.C. § 1205.
[68] 5 U.S.C. § 7513(a).
[69] 5 U.S.C. § 4303(a).
[70] 5 U.S.C. § 7701(c)(2)(B).
[71] 5 U.S.C. § 7701(b)(2)(A).
[72] 5 U.S.C. § 1212(c)(2).
[73] 5 U.S.C. § 1211(a). It provides that the Office of Special Counsel (OSC) will be headed by the Special Counsel and have a judicially noted official seal. The Senate report states that although the MSPB and the OSC had "separated themselves administratively in 1984," the whistleblower legislation "completes this process by establishing the OSC as an independent agency." S.Rept. 100-413 at 18. Moreover, the statute provides that the Special Counsel, appointed by the President, with the advice and consent of the Senate, may only be

removed from office for "inefficiency, neglect of duty, or malfeasance in office." 5 U.S.C. § 1211(b).

[74] 5 U.S.C. § 1212(a)(2).

[75] 5 U.S.C. § 1214(a)(5).

[76] 5 U.S.C. § 1213(c).

[77] 5 U.S.C. § 1214(b)(2).

[78] 5 U.S.C. § 1215(b).

[79] 5 U.S.C. § 1212(c).

[80] 5 U.S.C. § 1212(b)(1).

[81] In addition to investigating whether prohibited personnel actions have been taken because of protected whistleblowing disclosures, the WPA also charges the OSC with investigating whether there is a "substantial likelihood" that whistleblowing disclosures evidence violations of a law, rule or regulation. 5 U.S.C. §1213(b).

[82] 5 U.S.C. § 1214(b)(2)(A)(i).

[83] 5 U.S.C. § 1213(c)(2).

[84] 5 U.S.C. § 1213(c)(1).

[85] 5 U.S.C. § 1213(h).

[86] 5 U.S.C. § 1213(e)(2).

[87] 5 U.S.C. § 1213(e)(3).

[88] 5 U.S.C. § 1213(e)(1).

[89] 5 U.S.C. § 1213(g)(2).

[90] 5 U.S.C. § 1213(g)(1).

[91] 5 U.S.C. § 1213(f).

[92] 5 U.S.C. § 1214(a)(1)(C)(ii).

[93] 5 U.S.C. § 1214(a)(1)(D).

[94] 5 U.S.C. § 1214(b)(2)(B).

[95] 5 U.S.C. § 1214(b)(2)(C).

[96] 5 U.S.C. § 1214(b)(3).

[97] 5 U.S.C. §1214(b)(4)(i).

[98] 5 U.S.C. § 1214(c).

[99] 5 U.S.C. § 1214(b)(4)(B).

[100] 5 U.S.C. § 1215(a)(1).

[101] 5 U.S.C. § 1215(a)(2)(C).

[102] 5 U.S.C. § 1215(a)(3).

[103] 5 U.S.C. § 1204(m)(1).

[104] 5 U.S.C. § 1215(b).

[105] 5 U.S.C. § 1212(c).

[106] 5 U.S.C. § 1214(b)(1)(A)(i),(ii).

[107] 5 U.S.C. § 1214(b)(1)(A)(iii).

[108] 5 U.S.C. § 1214(b)(1)(B),(C).

[109] 5 U.S.C. § 1214(b)(1)(D).

[110] 5 U.S.C. §§ 1221, 1214(a)(3).

[111] 5 U.S.C. § 7701.

[112] 5 U.S.C. § 1221(j).

[113] 5 U.S.C. § 1221(g)(1)(A)(i),(ii).

[114] 5 U.S.C. § 1221(g)(1)(B).

[115] 5 U.S.C. § 1221(e)(1).

[116] 5 U.S.C. § 1212(c)(2).

In: Whistleblower Protections
Editor: Daryl R. Arcelloni

ISBN: 978-1-62417-211-3

Chapter 2

THE WHISTLEBLOWER PROTECTION ACT: AN OVERVIEW*

L. Paige Whitaker

SUMMARY

This report discusses the federal statutory protections contained within the Whistleblower Protection Act (WPA) for federal employees who engage in "whistleblowing," that is, making a disclosure evidencing illegal or improper government activities. The protections of the WPA apply to most federal executive branch employees and become applicable where a "personnel action" is taken "because of" a "protected disclosure" made by a "covered employee." Generally, whistleblower protections may be raised within four forums or proceedings: (1) employee appeals to the Merit Systems Protection Board of an agency's adverse action against an employee, known as "Chapter 77" appeals; (2) actions instituted by the Office of Special Counsel; (3) individually maintained rights of action before the Merit Systems Protection Board (known as an individual right of action, or IRA); and (4) grievances brought by the employee under negotiated grievance procedures.

---

* This is an edited, reformatted and augmented version of a Congressional Research Service publication, CRS Report for Congress RL33918, prepared for Members and Committees of Congress, from www.crs.gov, dated March 12, 2007.

On March 9, 2007, the House Committee on Oversight and Government Reform reported H.R. 985 (110th Cong.) H.Rept. 110-42, the Whistleblower Protection Enhancement Act of 2007, which would amend the WPA by providing protections for certain national security, government contractor, and science-based agency whistleblowers, and by enhancing the existing whistleblower protections for all federal employees.

Introduction and Background

The Whistleblower Protection Act (WPA) provides statutory protections for federal employees who engage in "whistleblowing," that is, making a disclosure evidencing illegal or improper government activities. The protections of the WPA apply to most federal executive branch employees and become applicable when a "personnel action" is taken "because of" a "protected disclosure" made by a "covered employee." Generally, whistleblower protections may be raised within four forums or proceedings: (1) employee appeals to the Merit Systems Protection Board of an agency's adverse action against an employee, known as "Chapter 77" appeals; (2) actions instituted by the Office of Special Counsel; (3) individually maintained rights of action before the Merit Systems Protection Board (known as an individual right of action, or IRA); and (4) grievances brought by the employee under negotiated grievance procedures.

When Congress first enacted the Whistleblower Protection Act (WPA) in 1989, it stated that the intent of the legislation was to:

> strengthen and improve protection for the rights of Federal employees, to prevent reprisals, and to help eliminate wrongdoing within the Government by — (1) mandating that employees should not suffer adverse consequences as a result of prohibited personnel practices; and (2) establishing ... that while disciplining those who commit prohibited personnel practices may be used as a means by which to help accomplish that goal, the protection of individuals who are the subject of prohibited personnel practices remains the paramount consideration.[1]

The operative statutory protections of the WPA are embodied in its definition of "prohibited personnel practices":

> § 2302. Prohibited personnel practices
> (b) Any employee who has authority to take, direct others to take, recommend, or approve any personnel action, shall not, with respect to such authority — ... (8) take or fail to take, or threaten to take or fail to take, a personnel action with respect to any employee or applicant for employment because of —
> (A) any disclosure of information by an employee or applicant which the employee or applicant reasonably believes evidences — (i) a violation of any law, rule, or regulation, or (ii) gross mismanagement, a gross waste of funds, an abuse of authority, or a substantial and specific danger to public health or safety, if such disclosure is not specifically prohibited by law and if such information is not specifically required by Executive Order to be kept secret in the interest of national defense or the conduct of foreign affairs; or
> (B) any disclosure to the Special Counsel, or to the Inspector General of an agency or another employee designated by the head of the agency to receive such disclosures, of information which the employee or applicant reasonably believes evidences — (i) a violation of any law, rule, or regulation, or (ii) gross mismanagement, a gross waste of funds, an abuse of authority, or a substantial and specific danger to public health or safety;[2]

Essential Elements Triggering Application of the Whistleblower Protection Act (WPA)

In order to trigger the protections of the WPA, a case must contain the following elements: a *personnel action* that was taken *because of a protected disclosure* made by a *covered employee*.[3]

Covered Employees

Although anyone may disclose whistleblowing information to the Special Counsel for referral to the appropriate agency, the Special Counsel may order an investigation and require a report from the head of the agency only if the information is received from a "covered employee." In addition, with few exceptions, prohibited personnel practices apply only to covered employees. Hence, as a threshold matter, it is important to note which federal employees are statutorily covered.

Generally, current employees, former employees, or applicants for employment to positions in the executive branch of government in both the competitive and the excepted service, as well as positions in the Senior Executive Service, are considered covered employees.[4] However, those positions that are excepted from the competitive service because of their "confidential, policy-determining, policy-making, or policy-advocating character,"[5] and any positions exempted by the President based on a determination that it is necessary and warranted by conditions of good administration,[6] are not protected by the whistleblower statute. Moreover, the statute does not apply to federal workers employed by the Postal Service or the Postal Rate Commission,[7] the Government Accountability Office, the Federal Bureau of Investigation, the Central Intelligence Agency, the Defense Intelligence Agency, the National Imagery and Mapping Agency,[8] the National Security Agency, and any other executive entity that the President determines primarily conducts foreign intelligence or counter-intelligence activities.[9]

Protected Disclosures

"[A]ny disclosure of information" that a covered employee "reasonably believes" evidences "a violation of any law, rule, or regulation" or evidences "gross mismanagement, a gross waste of funds, an abuse of authority, or a substantial and specific danger to public health or safety" is protected on the condition that the disclosure is not prohibited by law nor required to be kept secret by Executive Order.[10] Moreover, "any disclosure" made to the Special Counsel or to the Inspector General of an agency or another employee designated by the head of the agency to receive such disclosures, which the employee "reasonably believes" evidences "a violation of any law, rule, or regulation," or evidences "gross mismanagement, a gross waste of funds, an abuse of authority, or a substantial and specific danger to public health or safety" is also protected.[11] Agency heads are required to inform their employees of these protections.[12]

Any Disclosure of Information. The WPA expressly provides that "any disclosure of information" is protected. With enactment of the WPA, Congress amended its statutory predecessor, the Civil Service Reform Act (CSRA).[13] In so doing, it changed the phrase "a disclosure" to "any disclosure," emphasizing the point that the courts, the OSC, and the MSPB should not erect barriers to disclosures that will limit the necessary flow of information from employees with information of government wrongdoing.[14] In the Committee Report accompanying the WPA legislation, the Senate specifically criticized a 1986 decision by the U.S. Court of Appeals for the Federal Circuit, *Fiorello v. Department of Justice*,[15] where an employee's disclosures were found not to be protected because the employee's "primary motivation" was not for the public good, but rather was for personal reasons.[16] The court reached this conclusion despite a lack of any indication in the Civil Service Reform Act that employee motives were relevant to deciding whether a disclosure is protected.[17]

Following enactment of the WPA in 1989, case law did not reflect the statutory expansion of "a disclosure" to "any disclosure." This lack of responsiveness by the courts and the MSPB was one factor prompting Congress in 1994 to amend the whistleblower statute. As the House report accompanying the 1994 amendments notes:

> Perhaps the most troubling precedents involve the Board's inability to understand that "any" means "any." The WPA protects "any" disclosure evidencing a reasonable belief of specified misconduct, a cornerstone to which the MSPB remains blind. The only restrictions are for classified information or material the release of which is specifically prohibited by statute. Employees must disclose that type of information through confidential channels to maintain protection; otherwise there are no exceptions.[18]

Reasonable Belief. For a disclosure to be protected, an employee must have a "reasonable belief" that the information is true. This is substantially a good faith requirement. In theory, the actual veracity of any disclosure does not affect whether a disclosure is protected.[19] In addition, for those disclosures enumerated under section 2302(b)(8)(A) that do not have to be kept confidential, the statute does not specify to whom the disclosures must be made in order to qualify as protected.[20]

Subject Matter of Disclosure. The statutory language of the whistleblower protections requires the disclosure to (a) evidence (i) a violation of any law, rule, or regulation, or (ii) gross mismanagement, a gross waste of funds, an abuse of authority, or a substantial and specific danger to public health or safety; and (b) not be prohibited by law or Executive Order, except when the disclosure is made to the Special Counsel or to the Inspector General of an agency or another employee designated by the head of the agency to receive such disclosures.[21]

The WPA limits evidence of mismanagement to only "gross" mismanagement.

As explained in the accompanying Senate report,

> While the Committee is concerned about improving the protection of whistleblowers, it is also concerned about the exhaustive administrative and judicial remedies provided under S. 508 that could be used by employees who have made disclosures of trivial matters. CSRA specifically established a de minimis standard for disclosures affecting the waste of funds by defining such disclosures as protected only if they involved "a gross waste of funds." Under S. 508, the Committee establishes a similar de minimis standard for disclosures of mismanagement by protecting them only if they involve "gross mismanagement."[22]

Moreover, whistleblowing disclosures that are made public must not contain information the disclosure of which is prohibited by law or which is prohibited by an Executive Order in the interest of national defense or the conduct of foreign affairs.[23] Disclosures that are otherwise "protected" disclosures may be made, however, regardless of statutory Executive Order secrecy requirements, to the Special Counsel or to an Inspector General of an agency or to an employee designated by the agency head to receive disclosures.[24]

Disclosures to Members of Congress. The WPA expressly provides that the statute is "not to be construed to authorize ... the taking of any personnel action against an employee who discloses information to the Congress."[25] With this provision of the law, Congress sought to protect its right to receive even "confidential" information from federal employees, without employee fear of reprisals:

> The provision is intended to make clear that by placing limitations on the kinds of information any employee may publicly disclose without suffering reprisal, there is not intent to limit the information an employee

may provide to Congress or to authorize reprisal against an employee for providing information to Congress. For example, 18 U.S.C. 1905 prohibits public disclosure of information involving trade secrets. That statute does not apply to transmittal of such information by an agency to Congress. Section 2302(b)(8) of this act would not protect an employee against reprisal for public disclosure of such statutorily protected information, but it is not to be inferred that an employee is similarly unprotected if such disclosure is made to the appropriate unit of the Congress. Neither title I nor any other provision of the act should be construed as limiting in any way the rights of employees to communicate with or testify before Congress.[26]

Personnel Actions

The WPA protects employees from reprisals in the form of an agency taking or failing to take a "personnel action." This encompasses a broad range of actions by an agency having a negative or adverse impact on the employee. The statute specifically defines the term "personnel action" to include 11 areas of agency activity:

(2) For the purpose of this section — (A) "personnel action" means —

I. an appointment;
II. a promotion;
III. an action under chapter 75 of this title or other disciplinary or corrective action;
IV. a detail, transfer, or reassignment;
V. a reinstatement;
VI. a restoration;
VII. a reemployment;
VIII. a performance evaluation under chapter 43 of this title;
IX. a decision concerning pay, benefits, or awards, or concerning education or training if the education or training may reasonably be expected to lead to an appointment, promotion, performance evaluation, or other action described in this subparagraph;
X. a decision to order psychiatric testing or examination; and
XI. any other significant change in duties, responsibilities, or working conditions;

> with respect to an employee in, or applicant for, a covered position in an agency, and in the case of an alleged prohibited personnel practice described in subsection (b)(8), an employee or applicant for employment in a Government corporation as defined in section 9101 of title 31.[27]

The final category, (xi), of covered personnel actions was intended to embrace significant actions or changes that, in relation to an employee's overall duties, responsibilities, or working conditions, are inconsistent with his or her professional qualifications, training, grade, or rank. The conference report accompanying WPA provided a detailed discussion of the types of actions that may fall within or be excluded from the final category of personnel actions:

> To be covered under this provision a personnel action must be significant, but it need not be expected to result in a reduction in pay or grade. It must also be inconsistent with an employee's salary or grade level. Thus, for example, if an individual is currently employed and assigned duties or responsibilities consistent with the individual's professional training or qualifications for the job, it would constitute a personnel action if the individual were detailed, transferred, or reassigned so that the employee's new overall duties or responsibilities were inconsistent with the individual's professional training or qualifications. Or, if an individual holding decisionmaking responsibilities or supervisory authority found that such responsibilities or authority were reduced so that the employee's responsibilities were inconsistent with his or her salary or grade level, such an action could constitute a personnel action within the meaning of this subsection. This is not intended to interfere with management's authority to assign individuals in accordance with available work, the priorities of the agency, and the needs of the agency for individuals with particular skills or to establish supervisory relationships. Moreover, it is the overall nature of the individual's responsibilities and duties that is the critical factor. The mere fact that a particular aspect of an individual's job assignment has been changed would not constitute a personnel action, without some showing that there has been a significant impact as described above on the overall nature or quality of his responsibilities or duties.[28]

Nexus Between a Protected Disclosure and a Personnel Action

The WPA changed the CSRA's definition of prohibited reprisals against whistleblowers in such a manner that personnel actions taken "because of" protected conduct are prohibited, rather than personnel actions taken "as a reprisal for" protected conduct, as the original statute provided. The amendment was made because the phrase, "as a reprisal for" had been interpreted to require a showing of an improper, retaliatory motive on the part of the acting official.[29] Indeed, two disciplinary action cases decided prior to the enactment of the WPA, *Starrett v. Special Counsel*[30] and *Harvey v. M.S.P.B.*,[31] required employees to show proof of the acting official's state of mind. These cases stand for the proposition that reprisal will not be found even if an agency's actions against an employee were based on factors arising from protected whistleblowing activities, so long as the agency officials were motivated by valid management reasons and not by any intent to "punish" the employee.[32] With the definition of "because of," Congress intended that a showing of the official's state of mind is no longer required. As stated in the Senate report accompanying the WPA legislation, "[r]egardless of the official's motives, personnel actions against employees should quite simply not be based on protected activities such as whistleblowing."[33] The WPA also expanded the CSRA definition of prohibited reprisal against whistleblowers to include "threats to take or fail to take" a personnel action against a whistleblower.[34]

OTHER PROTECTED ACTIVITIES

The WPA also expressly protects employees from prohibited personnel practices taken because they engaged in activities that are often related to whistleblowing, including testifying for others or lawfully assisting others exercise any appeal, complaint, or grievance right;[35] cooperating with or disclosing information to an Inspector General or Special Counsel;[36] or for refusing to obey an order that would violate the law.[37] In addition, employees are also protected from prohibited personnel practices taken because they exercised any appeal, complaint, or grievance right granted by any law, rule, or regulation.[38]

FORUMS WHERE WHISTLEBLOWER PROTECTIONS MAY BE RAISED

There are four general forums or proceedings where whistleblower protections may be raised: (A) in employee appeals to the Merit Systems Protection Board (MSPB) of an agency's adverse action against the employee, known as "Chapter 77" appeals;[39] (B) in actions instituted by the Office of Special Counsel (OSC);[40] (C) in individual rights of action;[41] and (D) in grievances brought by the employee under negotiated grievance procedures.[42] As a result of the 1994 WPA amendments, an aggrieved employee affected by a prohibited personnel action is precluded from choosing more than one of the above remedies.[43]

"Chapter 77" Appeals

The MSPB is authorized to hear and rule on appeals by employees regarding agency actions affecting the employee and which are appealable to the Board by law, rule, or regulation.[44] Types of agency actions against employees that are appealable to the MSPB and in which an employee may raise the defense of reprisal for whistleblowing as a "prohibited personnel practice" include adverse actions against the employee for "such cause as will promote the efficiency of the service" (generally referred to as conduct-based adverse actions),[45] and performance-based adverse actions against employees for "unacceptable performance."[46] In such appeals, an agency's decision and action will not be upheld if the employee "shows that the decision was based on any prohibited personnel practice described in section 2302(b) of this title."[47] If the MSPB finds that an employee or applicant for employment has prevailed in an appeal, the employee or applicant may be provided with interim relief, pending the outcome of any petition of review.[48] Moreover, the Special Counsel may not intervene in a "Chapter 77" appeal without the consent of the individual bringing the appeal.[49]

Actions by the Office of Special Counsel (OSC)

The WPA established the OSC as an agency independent from the MSPB.[50] Its primary responsibilities, however, have remained essentially the same as set forth in its statutory predecessor, the CSRA. With the goal of protecting employees, former employees, and applicants for employment from prohibited personnel practices, the OSC has the duty to receive allegations of prohibited personnel practices and to investigate such allegations,[51] as well as to conduct an investigation of possible prohibited personnel practices on its own initiative, absent any allegation.[52]

The Special Counsel has several avenues available through which to pursue allegations, complaints, and evidences of reprisals for whistleblowing activities, including (1) requiring agency investigations and agency reports concerning actions the agency is planning to take to rectify those matters referred;[53] (2) seeking an order for "corrective action" by the agency before the MSPB;[54] (3) seeking "disciplinary action" against officers and employees who have committed prohibited personnel practices;[55] (4) intervening in any proceedings before the MSPB, except that in cases where an individual has brought an individual right of action (IRA) under Section 1221 or a Chapter 77 appeal, the OSC must first obtain the individual's consent;[56] and (5) seeking a stay from the MSPB for any personnel action pending an investigation.[57]

Investigations.[58] Within 240 days of receipt of a complaint, the OSC must make a determination as to whether there are reasonable grounds to believe that a prohibited personnel practice has occurred, exists, or is to be taken.[59] If a positive determination is made and the information was sent to the Special Counsel by an employee, former employee, applicant for employment, or an employee who obtained the information acting within the scope of employment,[60] the Special Counsel must transmit the information to the appropriate agency head and require that the agency head conduct an investigation and submit a written report.[61] The identity of the complaining employee may not be disclosed without such individual's consent, unless the Special Counsel determines that disclosure is necessary to avoid imminent danger to health and safety or an imminent criminal violation.[62] The Special Counsel then reviews the reports as to their completeness and the reasonableness of the findings[63] and submits the reports to Congress, the President, the Comptroller General,[64] and the complainant.[65]

If the Special Counsel does not make a positive determination, however, he or she may only transmit the information to the agency head with the consent of the individual.[66] Further, if the Special Counsel receives the information from some source other than the ones described above, he or she *may* transmit the information to the appropriate agency head who shall inform the Special Counsel of any action taken.[67] In any case evidencing a criminal violation, however, all information is referred to the Attorney General and no report is transmitted to the complainant.[68]

Throughout its investigation, the OSC must give notice of the status of the investigation to the individual who brought the allegation. The 1994 WPA amendments changed the period of this notification from 90 to 60 days.69 In addition, no later than 10 days before the termination of an investigation, a written status report including the proposed findings and legal conclusions must be made to the individual who made the allegation of wrongdoing.[70]

Corrective Actions. If in any investigation the Special Counsel determines that there are "reasonable grounds to believe" a prohibited personnel practice exists or has occurred, the Special Counsel must report findings and recommendations, and may include recommendations for corrective action, to the MSPB, the agency involved, the Office of Personnel Management and, optionally, to the President.[71] If the agency does not act to correct the prohibited personnel practice, the Special Counsel may petition the MSPB for corrective action.[72] The MSPB, before rendering its decision, is required to provide an opportunity for oral or written comments by the Special Counsel, the agency involved and the Office of Personnel Management, and for written comments by any individual who alleges to be the victim of the prohibited personnel practices.[73]

The WPA made it easier for a complainant to prove retaliation for whistleblowing in a corrective action before the MSPB. The Special Counsel need only prove by a preponderance of the evidence that the disclosure was a "contributing factor" in the personnel action, instead of a "significant factor."[74] In addition, once the MSPB renders a final order or decision of corrective action, complainants have the right to judicial review in the U.S. Court of Appeals for the Federal Circuit.[75]

In what is probably the most significant change from its statutory predecessor, the CSRA, the WPA increased the standard by which an agency must prove its affirmative defense that it would have taken the personnel action even if the employee had not engaged in protected conduct. Once the complainant's *prima facie* case of reprisal has been established by showing that the whistleblowing was a contributing factor in the personnel action, the government is required to demonstrate by "clear and convincing evidence" that it would have taken the same personnel action even in the absent of such disclosure.[76] Under the CSRA, the government's standard of proof was a "preponderance of the evidence." "Clear and convincing evidence," although a lesser standard than the criminal standard of "beyond a reasonable doubt," is greater than "preponderance of the evidence."

Disciplinary Actions. Proceedings for disciplinary action against an officer or employee who commits a prohibited personnel practice may be instituted by the Special Counsel by filing a written complaint with the MSPB.[77] After proceedings before the MSPB or an administrative law judge,[78] if violations are found, the MSPB may impose any of various disciplinary actions, including removal, reduction in grade, debarment from federal employment for a period not to exceed five years, suspension, reprimand, or an assessment of civil fines up to $1,000.[79] In addition, the agency involved may be held responsible for reasonable attorney's fees.[80] In the case of presidentially appointed and Senate confirmed employees in "confidential, policy-making, policy-determining, or policy-advocating" positions, the complaint and the statement of facts, along with any response from the employee, are to be presented to the President for disposition in lieu of the presentation to the Board.[81] The OSC may recommend, to the appropriate federal agency head, disciplinary action against members of the uniformed services or contractor personnel who have engaged in a prohibited personnel practice against a federal employee.[82]

Intervention. As a matter of right, the Special Counsel may intervene or otherwise participate in any proceedings before the MSPB, except that in cases where an individual has brought an individual right of action (IRA) under Section 1221 or a Chapter 77 appeal, the OSC must first obtain the individual's consent.[83]

Stays. Upon application by the OSC, a member of the MSPB may "stay" or postpone, for 45 days, pending an investigation, a personnel action that the Special Counsel has reasonable grounds to believe constitutes a prohibited personnel practice, unless the member determines that a stay would not be appropriate under the circumstances.[84] If no MSPB member acts within three days of the OSC application, the stay becomes effective.[85] After the employing agency has had an opportunity to comment on the appropriateness of extending a stay, the MSPB may extend it.[86] A stay may be terminated by the MSPB at any time, except that a stay may not be terminated by the MSPB on its own motion or on the motion of an agency, unless notice and opportunity for oral or written comments are first provided to the Special Counsel and the individual on whose behalf the stay was ordered; or on a motion of the Special Counsel, unless notice and opportunity for oral or written comments are first provided to the individual on whose behalf the stay was ordered.[87]

Individual Right of Action (IRA)

The WPA provides that an employee, former employee, or applicant for employment has the independent right to seek review of whistleblower reprisal cases by the MSPB 60 days after the OSC closes an investigation or 120 days after filing a complaint with the OSC.[88] As a result of the IRA statutory provisions, a greater number of employees, including probationers, temporaries, and excepted service, have a method of appeal to the MSPB for whistleblower reprisals that was not previously available under the CSRA.[89] In addition, retired employees are not barred from instituting this type of appeal.[90] If the employee is the prevailing party before the MSPB, based on the finding of a prohibited personnel practice, or if the employee is the prevailing party in an appeal to the MSPB, regardless of the basis of the decision, the WPA provides several remedies. These may include placing the individual, as nearly as possible, in the position the individual would have been in had the prohibited personnel practice not occurred, awarding back pay and related benefits, recompensing medical costs incurred, travel expenses, or any other reasonable and foreseeable consequential charges.[91] In all cases, corrective action includes awarding attorneys' fees.[92] As a result of the 1994 WPA amendments, the MSPB findings can be based on circumstantial evidence.[93] Moreover, the Special Counsel may not intervene in an individual right of action without the consent of the individual bringing the appeal.[94]

Negotiated Grievance Procedures

Beyond the statutory provisions of the WPA, the fourth general forum where the defense or claim of reprisal for whistleblowing activities may be raised is a grievance proceeding initiated by an employee pursuant to a grievance procedure that was negotiated through collective bargaining between the employee's agency and the employee union representing employees of the agency.[95] The federal statutory provisions for grievance procedures note that certain actions that may be pursued either in a grievance proceeding or by other statutory means, such as discrimination complaints referenced under 5 U.S.C. § 2302(b)(1) or appeals of adverse actions for "conduct" or "performance,"[96] may only be pursued in one forum or the other, but not through both.[97]

Selection of the negotiated procedure does not, however, prejudice the right of an aggrieved employee to request that the MSPB review the final decision in the case of any personnel action that could have been appealed to the Board; or, where applicable, to request that the Equal Employment Opportunity Commission (EEOC) review a final decision in any other matter involving a complaint of discrimination of the type prohibited by any law administered by the EEOC.[98]

SUMMARY OF THE WHISTLEBLOWER PROTECTION ENHANCEMENT ACT OF 2007 (H.R. 985, 110TH CONGRESS)

On February 12, 2007, Representatives Waxman, Platts, Van Hollen, and T. Davis introduced H.R. 985 (110th Cong.), the Whistleblower Protection Enhancement Act of 2007, which on March 9, the House Committee on Oversight and Government Reform reported with amendments (H.Rept. 110-42), and placed on the legislative calendar.

H.R. 985 would amend the WPA to extend whistleblower protections to federal employees who specialize in national security issues. While current law expressly exempts employees of certain agencies relating to national security, Section 10 of the bill extends whistleblower protections to employees of the Federal Bureau of Investigation, the Central Intelligence Agency, the Defense Intelligence Agency, the National Geospatial-Intelligence Agency, the National Security Agency, and the National Reconnaissance Office and "any other Executive agency, or element or unit thereof, determined by the President ... to have as its principal function the conduct of foreign intelligence or counterintelligence activities." Likewise, Section 11 of the bill would extend whistleblower protections to employees of companies with government contracts.

Current law defines "disclosures" covered by the WPA to include information evidencing an abuse of authority. Section 13 of the bill would extend WPA protections to employees of science-based agencies by providing that "abuse of authority" includes "any action that compromises the validity or accuracy of federally funded research and analysis" and "the dissemination of false or misleading scientific, medical, or technical information."

Section 3 of the bill would clarify that "any" disclosure regarding waste, fraud, or abuse means that the WPA applies to such disclosures "without restriction as to time, place, form, motive, context, or prior disclosure" and includes formal and informal communication. Section 4 of the bill would provide that an employee covered by the WPA can rebut the presumption that a federal official performed his or her duties in accordance with the law by providing substantial evidence to the contrary. In addition, Section 9 of the bill would provide that such covered employees may bring an action for *de novo* review in the appropriate U.S. district court if the Merit Systems Protection Board (MSPB) does not take action on their claims within 180 days.

End Notes

[1] 5 U.S.C. § 1201 nt.
[2] 5 U.S.C. § 2302(b)(8).
[3] Id.
[4] 5 U.S.C. § 2302(a)(2)(B).
[5] 5 U.S.C. § 2302(a)(2)(B)(i).
[6] 5 U.S.C. § 2302(a)(2)(B)(ii).
[7] 5 U.S.C. § 2105(e).
[8] The Central Imagery Office was exempted from coverage with the passage of the 1994 WPA amendments. The agency was renamed the "National Imagery and Mapping Agency" with the passage of the National Defense Authorization Act for Fiscal Year 1997. P.L. 104- 201, § 1122(b)(1).
[9] 5 U.S.C. § 2302(a)(2)(C).
[10] 5 U.S.C. § 2302(b)(8)(A).
[11] 5 U.S.C. § 2302(b)(8)(B).
[12] 5 U.S.C. § 2302(c).
[13] Civil Service Reform Act of 1978, P.L. 95-454, 92 Stat. 1114.
[14] S.Rept. 100-413 (1988) at 13.
[15] 795 F.2d 1544 (Fed. Cir. 1986).
[16] S.Rept. 100-413 (1988) at 13.
[17] Id.
[18] H.Rept. 103-769 (1994) at 18.
[19] S.Rept. 100-413 (1988) at 12.
[20] Id.
[21] 2 U.S.C. §2302(b)(8)(A).
[22] S.Rept. 100-413, supra at 12.
[23] 5 U.S.C. § 2302(b)(8).
[24] Id.
[25] 5 U.S.C. § 2302(b). See also 5 U.S.C. § 7211, providing that an employee is guaranteed the right to freely petition or furnish information to Congress, a Member of Congress, a committee, or a Member thereof.
[26] H.Rept. 95-1717 (Conference Report) (1978), reprinted in 1978 U.S. CODE CONG. & AD. NEWS 2861.
[27] 5 U.S.C. § 2302(a)(2)(A).
[28] H.Rept. 95-1717 (Conference Report)(1978) at 128, 129-130, reprinted in 1978 U.S. CODE CONG. & AD. NEWS 2861.
[29] S.Rept. 100-13 (1988).

[30] 792 F.2d 1246 (4th Cir. 1986).
[31] 802 F.2d 537 (D.C. Cir. 1986).
[32] S.Rept. 100-413 (1988) at 15.
[33] Id. at 16.
[34] Id.
[35] 5 U.S.C. § 2302(b)(9)(B).
[36] 5 U.S.C. § 2302(b)(9)(C).
[37] 5 U.S.C. § 2302(b)(9)(D).
[38] 5 U.S.C. § 2302(b)(9)(A).
[39] 5 U.S.C. § 7701.
[40] 5 U.S.C. §§ 1211-1215.
[41] 5 U.S.C. § 1221.
[42] 5 U.S.C. § 7121.
[43] See 5 U.S.C. § 7121(g)(2).
[44] 5 U.S.C. § 7701, 5 U.S.C. § 1205.
[45] 5 U.S.C. § 7513(a). See 5 U.S.C. § 7513(d) as to appealability under § 7701.
[46] 5 U.S.C. § 4303(a). See 5 U.S.C. § 4303(e) as to appealability to the MSPB under § 7701.
[47] 5 U.S.C. § 7701(c)(2)(B).
[48] 5 U.S.C. § 7701(b)(2)(A).
[49] 5 U.S.C. § 1212(c)(2).
[50] 5 U.S.C. § 1211(a). This section established the Office of Special Counsel (OSC), and provided that it will be headed by the Special Counsel and have a judicially noted official seal. The Senate report states that although the MSPB and the OSC had "separated themselves administratively in 1984," the whistleblower legislation "completes this process by establishing the OSC as an independent agency." S.Rept. 100-413 at 18. Moreover, the statute provides that the Special Counsel, appointed by the President, with the advice and consent of the Senate, may only be removed from office for "inefficiency, neglect of duty, or malfeasance in office." 5 U.S.C. § 1211(b).
[51] 5 U.S.C. § 1212(a)(2).
[52] 5 U.S.C. § 1214(a)(5).
[53] 5 U.S.C. § 1213(c).
[54] 5 U.S.C. § 1214(b)(2).
[55] 5 U.S.C. § 1215(b).
[56] 5 U.S.C. § 1212(c).
[57] 5 U.S.C. § 1212(b)(1).
[58] In addition to investigating whether prohibited personnel actions have been taken because of protected whistleblowing disclosures, the WPA also charges the OSC with investigating whether there is a "substantial likelihood" that whistleblowing disclosures evidence violations of a law, rule or regulation. See 5 U.S.C. §1213(b).
[59] 5 U.S.C. § 1214(b)(2)(A)(i).
[60] 5 U.S.C. § 1213(c)(2).
[61] 5 U.S.C. § 1213(c)(1).
[62] 5 U.S.C. § 1213(h).
[63] 5 U.S.C. § 1213(e)(2).
[64] 5 U.S.C. § 1213(e)(3).
[65] 5 U.S.C. § 1213(e)(1).
[66] 5 U.S.C. § 1213(g)(2).
[67] 5 U.S.C. § 1213(g)(1).

[68] 5 U.S.C. § 1213(f).
[69] 5 U.S.C. § 1214(a)(1)(C)(ii).
[70] 5 U.S.C. § 1214(a)(1)(D).
[71] 5 U.S.C. § 1214(b)(2)(B).
[72] 5 U.S.C. § 1214(b)(2)(C).
[73] 5 U.S.C. § 1214(b)(3).
[74] 5 U.S.C. §1214(b)(4)(i).
[75] 5 U.S.C. § 1214(c).
[76] 5 U.S.C. § 1214(b)(4)(B).
[77] 5 U.S.C. § 1215(a)(1).
[78] 5 U.S.C. § 1215(a)(2)(C).
[79] 5 U.S.C. § 1215(a)(3).
[80] 5 U.S.C. § 1204(m)(1).
[81] 5 U.S.C. § 1215(b).
[82] 5 U.S.C. §1215(c)(1).
[83] 5 U.S.C. § 1212(c).
[84] 5 U.S.C. § 1214(b)(1)(A)(i),(ii).
[85] 5 U.S.C. § 1214(b)(1)(A)(iii).
[86] 5 U.S.C. § 1214(b)(1)(B),(C).
[87] 5 U.S.C. § 1214(b)(1)(D).
[88] 5 U.S.C. § 1221(a).
[89] See 5 U.S.C. § 7701.
[90] 5 U.S.C. § 1221(j).
[91] 5 U.S.C. § 1221(g)(1)(A)(i),(ii).
[92] 5 U.S.C. § 1221(g)(1)(B).
[93] 5 U.S.C. § 1221(e)(1).
[94] 5 U.S.C. § 1212(c)(2).
[95] 5 U.S.C. § 7121.
[96] 5 U.S.C. §§ 4303 and 7512.
[97] 5 U.S.C. § 7121(d),(e).
[98] 5 U.S.C. § 7121(d).

In: Whistleblower Protections
Editor: Daryl R. Arcelloni

ISBN: 978-1-62417-211-3

Chapter 3

WHISTLEBLOWER PROTECTION: ACTIONS NEEDED TO IMPROVE DOD'S MILITARY WHISTLEBLOWER REPRISAL PROGRAM*

The United States Government Accountability Office

WHY GAO DID THIS STUDY

Whistleblowers help guard the federal government against waste, fraud, and abuse. The Military Whistleblower Protection Act provides servicemembers with a means to seek relief from reprisals and to hold subjects accountable. GAO was asked to determine the extent to which the Department of Defense (DOD) has (1) satisfied statutory timeliness requirements for processing military whistleblower reprisal cases, (2) established and implemented oversight mechanisms for its process, and (3) taken corrective action in cases where the DOD Inspector General (DODIG) substantiated reprisal claims. GAO also analyzed case characteristics. GAO examined laws, regulations, and guidance documents; interviewed officials from DODIG, service IGs, service Boards for the Correction of Military Records (BCMRs), and the Office of the Undersecretary of Defense for Personnel and Readiness; and collected and analyzed case data.

* This is an edited, reformatted and augmented version of The United States Government Accountability Office publication, Report to the Ranking Member, Committee on the Judiciary, U.S. Senate GAO-12-362, dated February 2012.

GAO also conducted a detailed file review using a representative sample of cases closed between January 1, 2009 and March 31, 2011.

WHAT GAO RECOMMENDS

GAO recommends that DOD implement procedures to track and report data on its case processing timeliness, take actions to improve oversight of its investigative process, and develop processes to ensure appropriate corrective actions are taken in substantiated cases. DOD concurred with all of GAO's recommendations.

WHAT GAO FOUND

DODIG has taken multiple steps, in collaboration with the service IGs in some instances, to improve DOD's ability to process military whistleblower reprisal cases in a timely manner. Timeliness is important to ensure the reliability of evidence and appropriate resolution of reprisal allegations. However, DODIG has generally not met statutory requirements to report on investigations within 180 days, or to provide alternative notification. DODIG has undertaken efforts to improve timeliness by, for example, eliminating a time-consuming phase of its investigative process. However, DOD's efforts are hampered by unreliable and incomplete data. For instance, GAO found that DODIG has not consistently or accurately recorded key dates to track how long investigations take to complete. Without key timeliness data, DODIG may have difficulty in identifying process areas requiring improvement and evaluating the impact of reforms. Further, the absence of this information limits congressional decision makers' ability to provide oversight of DOD's whistleblower reprisal investigative program.

DODIG has begun executing an action plan that includes acting on prior external and internal review recommendations in order to improve its oversight of the department's whistleblower reprisal process, but implementation of this plan is not yet complete and challenges exist in three areas:

- *Performance metrics.* DODIG has not yet established performance metrics to ensure the quality of reprisal investigations.

- *Guidance.* DOD's guidance related to the whistleblower program is outdated and does not reflect current investigative processes. Additionally, some of the guidance is unclear, leading to inconsistent implementation among the service IGs. Moreover, DODIG has not been consistently adhering to standards regarding the maintenance of its case files, resulting in generally incomplete files.
- *Case monitoring processes and procedures.* DODIG lacks standard case monitoring processes and procedures, which may hinder its ability to consistently maintain visibility and assess the status of outstanding reprisal investigations including those conducted by service and component IGs.

Until it further addresses the challenges it faces in regard to oversight mechanisms, DODIG cannot be assured that it is effectively conducting its oversight responsibilities or implementing the whistleblower reprisal program as intended.

DOD's efforts to ensure that appropriate corrective action is taken—both for whistleblowers and against those who reprise against whistleblowers—are hampered by disconnected investigative and corrective action processes and the limited visibility of the corrective actions taken. DODIG and the service BCMRs are not consistently identifying and tracking data on action taken to undo the reprisal damage done to whistleblowers. Further, unreliable data regarding corrective action taken against those found to have reprised against whistleblowers is hindering oversight of this key aspect of whistleblower protections. Without addressing these issues, whistleblowers may not be getting the full protection and resolution they deserve.

February 22, 2012

The Honorable Charles E. Grassley
Ranking Member,
Committee on the Judiciary
United States Senate

Whistleblowers play an important role in safeguarding the federal government against waste, fraud, and abuse, and their willingness to come forward can contribute to improvements in government operations. These whistleblowers also risk reprisals from their employers, sometimes being demoted, reassigned, or fired. In 1988, Congress enacted the Military

Whistleblower Protection Act,[1] which provides protections from reprisal for a servicemember who discloses information concerning, among other things, fraud, waste, and abuse to designated persons such as an inspector general (IG) or someone in the servicemember's chain of command.[2] Under this law, the Department of Defense (DOD) IG has final responsibility for approving the results of all investigations, although both DODIG and the service IGs can investigate allegations of reprisal.[3]

Despite the protections afforded to military whistleblowers under the Military Whistleblower Protection Act and subsequent amendments, concerns persisted that servicemembers were not being adequately protected by DOD's investigative process. In response, DODIG requested that the Department of Justice IG assess whether DODIG was properly and effectively discharging its statutory responsibilities to protect members of the Armed Forces from reprisal.[4] The resulting July 2009 report[5] highlighted timeliness in processing complaints as DOD's biggest challenge and made detailed recommendations for improvement based on the underlying report findings.

To assist Congress in providing oversight of DOD's efforts to protect military whistleblowers, you asked us to examine DOD's military whistleblower reprisal process. Specifically, this report examines the extent to which DOD has (1) satisfied statutory timeliness requirements for processing military whistleblower reprisal cases and what factors, if any, impact its ability to do so; (2) established and implemented oversight mechanisms for its military whistleblower reprisal process; and (3) taken corrective action in cases where DODIG substantiated military whistleblower reprisal claims. The report also identifies key characteristics of military whistleblower reprisal cases.

To address these objectives, we reviewed a random selection of case files retained by DODIG for military whistleblower reprisal cases closed between January 1, 2009 and March 31, 2011, to identify case characteristics, and address the extent to which DODIG met timeliness requirements and had oversight mechanisms in place.6 The margin of error associated with the confidence intervals of our case file review proportion estimates is no more than plus or minus 11 percentage points at the 95 percent level of confidence. The margin of error for any mean values based on our case file review will vary depending on the variability of the data and so is reported along with the mean. To address all our audit objectives, we also collected and analyzed data on all closed military whistleblower reprisal cases from DODIG,7 the headquarters-level IGs from the Army, Navy, Air Force, and Marine Corps,8 and the Boards for Correction of Military Records (BCMRs) of the Army,

Navy,9 and Air Force.10 We assessed the data we obtained and determined that the data we used were sufficiently reliable for our audit objectives. We also reviewed relevant laws, regulations and guidance documents, internal memos, reports, and briefings. Further, we interviewed officials from DODIG, the service headquarters IGs and service field IGs from the Army, Navy, Air Force, and Marine Corps, and the Army, Navy, and Air Force BCMRs, as well as the Office of the Under Secretary of Defense for Personnel and Readiness – Enterprise Services. We conducted this performance audit from April 2011 to February 2012 in accordance with generally accepted government auditing standards. Those standards require that we plan and perform the audit to obtain sufficient, appropriate evidence to provide a reasonable basis for our findings and conclusions based on our audit objectives. We believe that the evidence obtained provides a reasonable basis for our findings and conclusions based on our audit objectives. Additional details on our scope and methodology are discussed in more detail in appendix I.

BACKGROUND

The Military Whistleblower Protection Act of 1988, as amended, and its implementing directive, Department of Defense Directive 7050.06,[11] establish the basic concepts and framework for the investigative process and establish the roles and responsibilities of the various affected organizations. DODIG is the central organization for DOD's military whistleblower reprisal program and has a directorate responsible for investigations into military whistleblower reprisal allegations. This directorate also conducts or oversees investigations into allegations of improper referrals of servicemembers for mental health evaluations[12] and conducts investigations into reprisal allegations involving civilians, contractors, and nonappropriated fund employees,[13,14] although historically military whistleblower reprisal cases make up approximately 80 percent of its caseload. Under the law, the service IGs and other DOD component IGs[15] can also investigate military whistleblower reprisal allegations and make recommendations regarding the disposition of cases. However, DODIG is responsible for reviewing and approving the results of all investigations of military whistleblower reprisal allegations. DODIG publicly reports on its military whistleblower protection program activities in its required semiannual report to Congress, including consolidated data on all of the cases the reprisal directorate received and closed—numbers that include military whistleblower reprisal cases.[16]

Table 1. Roles and Responsibilities of Key Organizations and Individuals in the Military Whistleblower Reprisal Process

Organization or individuals	Roles and responsibilities
Complainant	• Military member who alleges that they have been reprised against for their whistleblower activities.
Subject or Responsible Management Official	• Individual who is alleged to have reprised against a whistleblower.
Secretaries of the Military Departments	Responsible for: • Ensuring that consideration of all military whistleblower allegations submitted under the Military Whistleblower Protection Act are thorough, objective, and timely, and that corrective actions are taken promptly.
Department of Defense Inspector General (DODIG)	Responsible for: • Directly receiving some whistleblower reprisal complaints, expeditiously conducting investigations. • Providing management and oversight of all military whistleblower reprisal investigations conducted by other IGs in DOD and the whistleblower reprisal investigative process in general. • Reviewing and approving all determinations reached by service IGs in military whistleblower reprisal investigations.
Service Inspectors General (IGs)	Inspectors General from the military services (Army, Navy, Air Force, Marine Corps) are responsible for: • Notifying the DODIG within 10 working days of receiving any whistleblower reprisal allegation. • Receiving, expeditiously investigating, and, if they choose, making recommendations on case disposition to DODIG.
Boards for the Correction of Military Records (BCMR)[a]	Military department organizations (Army, Air Force, Navy) with responsibility for: • Reviewing and taking action on applications for the correction of military records at the request of a complainant (the secretary of the military department concerned issues the final decision on the application). • Requesting, if they deem it necessary, that DODIG or the service IGs gather further evidence.
Office of the Under Secretary of Defense for Personnel and Readiness – Enterprise Services[b]	Organization within the Department of Defense responsible for: • Receiving information on all IG military whistleblower reprisal investigations that exceed 180 days as well as the results of full investigations. • Reviewing and making final decisions on behalf of the Secretary of Defense on appeals of BCMR whistleblower reprisal decisions.

Source: GAO analysis of DOD information.

[a] The Navy BCMR also reviews cases brought to it by members of the Marine Corps.

[b] DOD Directive 7050.06 (Jul. 23, 2007) assigns responsibility for the noted functions to the Deputy Under Secretary of Defense for Program Integration. In July 2010, the Under Secretary of Defense for Personnel and Readiness began to reorganize and realign Program Integration. On December 1, 2011, the Office of the Under Secretary of Defense for Personnel and Readiness (OUSD(P&R)) - Enterprise Services was designated as the successor organization for the Deputy Under Secretary of Defense for Program Integration.

A description of some of the key organizations and individuals and their roles in the military whistleblower reprisal process can be found in table 1.

The two basic components of a whistleblower reprisal allegation are the protected communication and the unfavorable personnel action. A protected communication is any lawful communication to a Member of Congress or an IG or a communication with appropriate officials about information that the servicemember reasonably believes evidences a violation of law or regulation, including a law or regulation prohibiting sexual harassment or unlawful discrimination, gross mismanagement, a gross waste of funds or other resources, an abuse of authority, or a substantial and specific danger to public health or safety.[17] A servicemember who makes or prepares to make a protected communication is considered a whistleblower. It is DOD's policy that servicemembers shall be free from reprisal for making or preparing to make a protected communication and that no person may take or threaten to take an unfavorable personnel action, such as an unfavorable performance evaluation, or withhold or threaten to withhold a favorable personnel action, such as granting a promotion or award, in reprisal for making or preparing to make a protected communication.[18]

To initiate an investigation under the Military Whistleblower Protection Act, a servicemember must typically make a reprisal allegation to an IG in DOD within 60 days of becoming aware of the personnel action alleged to have been taken in reprisal.19,20 Allegations can also come to an IG through a Member of Congress. Once a complaint has been filed, the investigating organization—typically a service IG or DODIG—conducts a review to determine if the complaint qualifies as a whistleblower reprisal under the law and should be fully investigated. DODIG can also assign cases it receives to a service or other component IG for investigation and will also investigate cases that were not filed with it if the case is of special interest to DODIG.21 If a complaint is fully investigated, the investigating organization writes a formal report of investigation that includes a determination of whether the complaint is substantiated or not substantiated. Such a report also receives at least one legal sufficiency review. Complaints that are not fully investigated do not necessarily include a formal report or a legal review. No determination, including a determination that a complaint does not merit a full investigation, is final until DODIG approves it. Even after a full investigation is completed that substantiates reprisal, servicemembers do not receive relief from the unfavorable personnel actions from IGs in DOD but instead must separately apply to their military department's Board for Correction of Military Records (BCMR). See figure 1 for the process currently used by DOD to investigate military whistleblower reprisal allegations. IGs at DOD assess each allegation in the complaint using four basic questions, which they refer to as the "Acid Test." According to DODIG's *Guide to Investigating Reprisal and Improper Referrals for Mental Health Evaluations*,[22] the four questions are:

1. Did the military member make or prepare a communication protected by statute?
2. Was an unfavorable personnel action taken or threatened, or was a favorable action withheld or threatened to be withheld following the protected communication?
3. Did the official(s) responsible for taking, withholding, or threatening the personnel action know about the protected communication?
4. Does the evidence establish that the personnel action would have been taken, withheld, or threatened if the protected communication had not been made?

Investigators must answer all four questions when conducting a full investigation, but cases can be closed before a full investigation if investigators, with DODIG approval, determine that the answers to the earlier questions indicate that a reprisal action was not taken against the complainant or that the complainant was not reprised against for making a protected communication (see fig. 2). For example, DODIG could close a case if it determined that there was no protected communication (question 1) or that an unfavorable personnel action occurred before the protected communication (question 2). According to DODIG's investigative guide, report conclusions are to be based on a "preponderance of the evidence" when assessing the four questions. The guide states that this standard requires that more weight is given to the most credible and convincing evidence and that evidence which demonstrates to the reader that it is more probable than not that the facts and circumstances occurred as set forth in the investigative report. Although the service IGs have the same basic investigative process as outlined above, each service has adapted process specifics to its own circumstances. Each service reviews and approves the investigations it conducts at the service's headquarter IG before forwarding them to DODIG for final approval. Table 2 outlines differences among the services and DODIG in how they investigate reprisal cases.

Appendix II provides more information on the characteristics of military whistleblower reprisal cases.

DODIG IS GENERALLY NOT MEETING TIMELINESS REQUIREMENTS AND IMPROVEMENT EFFORTS ARE HINDERED BY UNRELIABLE AND INCOMPLETE DATA

DODIG has taken multiple steps, in collaboration with the service IGs in some instances, to improve DOD's ability to process military whistleblower reprisal cases in a timely manner. However, DOD has generally not met statutory requirements to provide reports on completed investigations within 180 days of the date the allegation was made or alternatively, to provide notice to the complainant and the Secretary of Defense. The July 2009 Department of Justice IG report found that lingering investigations leave complainants without resolution to their concern and could hold up a potential promotion for a subject. In addition, DODIG's May 2011 review of its military whistleblower reprisal process raised concerns that some complainants withdrew their cases because of the length of time it takes to complete investigations.[23] Further, DOD's efforts to improve processing time have been hindered by unreliable and incomplete data. Moreover, DODIG does not report data on timeliness in its semiannual reports, thereby limiting the information Congress could use to provide oversight of the military whistleblower reprisal program.

DODIG Faces Challenges in the Timely Processing of Reprisal Cases

DODIG and the service IGs have faced challenges to processing military whistleblower reprisal cases in a timely manner which they attribute to staffing shortages and process inefficiencies. Although DODIG has taken multiple steps, in collaboration with the service IGs in some instances, to improve processing time, these efforts have not yet resulted in meeting the statutory requirement to provide reports on completed investigations within 180 days of the date the allegation was made.[24]

Timeliness is a key challenge and an important factor in completing quality investigations because, without timely resolutions, the reliability of evidence could suffer, and the careers of both the complainants and subjects could be negatively impacted.

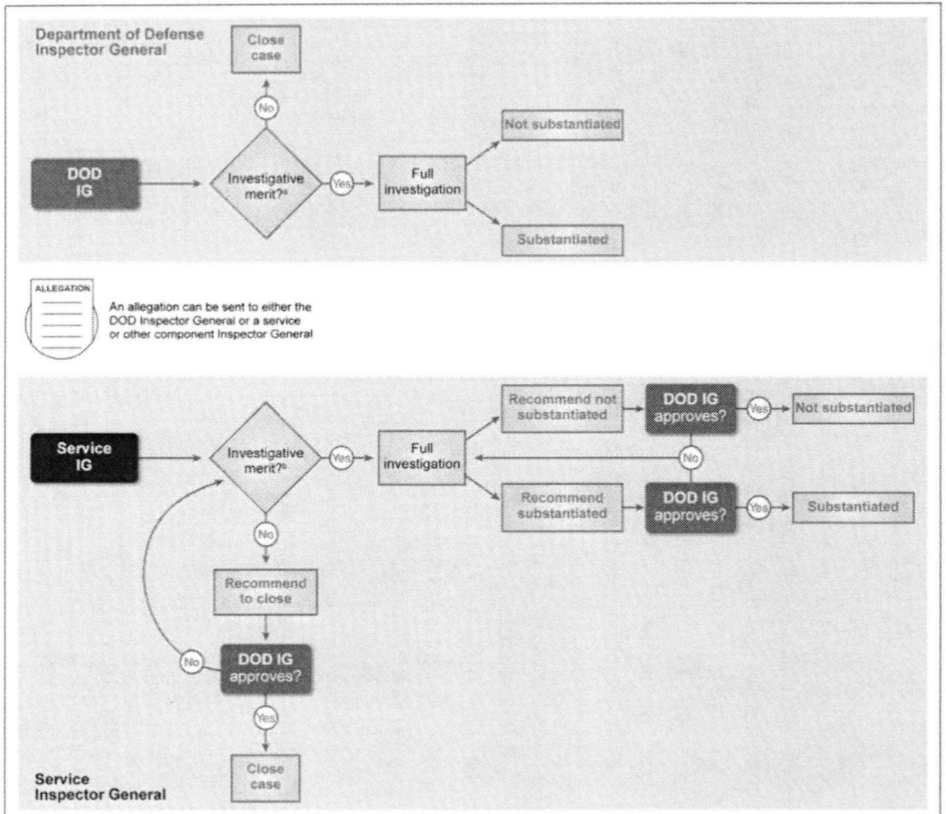

Source: GAO analysis of DOD information.

Notes: Since 2008, cases filed by servicemembers in the Army have undergone an initial review of investigative merit by DODIG. DODIG can also assign cases it receives to a service or component IG for investigation, and will also investigate cases that were not filed with it if the case is of special interest to DODIG.

[a] Currently, the determination of investigative merit by DODIG involves making an initial determination based on testimonial, and sometimes documentary evidence provided by the complainant.

[b] The determination of investigative merit for the service IGs spans a range and could be based on an assessment of the documents provided by the complainant but could also include a formal written report.

Figure 1. The Military Whistleblower Reprisal Investigative Process, as of January 2012.

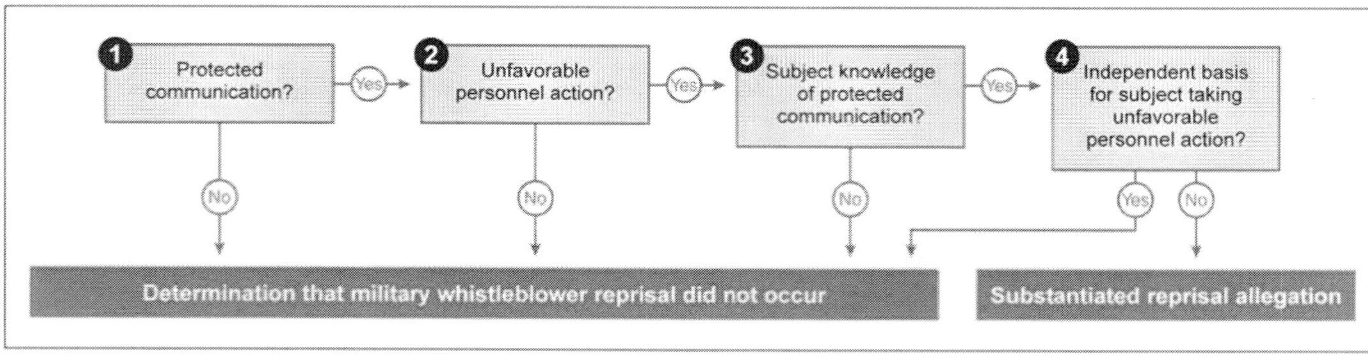

Source: GAO analysis of DOD information.

Figure 2. Acid Test for Military Whistleblower Reprisal Allegations.

Table 2. Reprisal Process Implementation Differences by Investigating Organization

	DODIG	Army[a]	Navy[a]	Marine Corps[a]	Air Force[a]
Level at which the investigation is conducted	DODIG conducts investigations and provides oversight and approval of all Service IG cases	Organization-level and above[b] with Army IG headquarters (HQ) oversight	Echelon II[c] Command level, with Navy IG HQ oversight	Marine Corps IG HQ	Wing level and above with Air Force IG HQ oversight
Number of legal reviews required for full investigations[d]	1 conducted at DODIG	1 required at the level where case is investigated	2; 1 conducted at Echelon II Command level and 1 required at Navy IG HQ	1 required at Marine Corps IG HQ level	2; 1 conducted at Major Command and 1 required at Air Force IG HQ
Investigator status	Primarily civilian	Primarily military	Primarily civilian	Civilian only	Mix depending on the level at which investigated
Mean number of cases closed per year by investigating organization[e]	66[f]	158	41	4	135
Active and reserve military servicemember population[g]	—	1,132,600	394,200	241,700	510,100

Source: GAO analysis of DOD information.

[a] The services investigate cases for both their active and reserve components.

[b] Army organizations—which are generally at the division level—have IGs assigned to them. These IGs are similar to installation-level IGs.

[c] Echelon II Commands have senior level of authority and report directly to the Chief of Naval Operations (CNO) and would be the equivalent of a major command.

[d] Based on requirements articulated by officials from the organizations noted. Additionally, both Navy and Marine Corps also require a legal sufficiency review for cases that do not go to full investigation.

[e] Mean number of cases closed per year by investigating organization based on data for all military whistleblower reprisal cases closed between fiscal year 2006 and the first half of fiscal year 2011 (October 1, 2005 through March 31, 2011).

[f] In addition to having conducted a mean of 66 investigations per year during this time period, DODIG also provided oversight reviews for the investigations completed by the service IGs.

[g] Active and reserve military servicemember population figures are the fiscal year 2011 estimates in DOD's Defense Manpower Requirements Report: Fiscal Year 2011 (December 2010).

DOD Directive 7050.06 addresses the need to conduct investigations expeditiously.[25] Officials at DODIG and the service IGs stated that staffing levels are a key factor in determining the timely processing of reprisal cases. According to DODIG, the military whistleblower reprisal caseload has grown significantly since the enactment of the Military Whistleblower Protection Act, and staffing has not kept up with the increased caseload. Further, service IG officials told us that DODIG's review of service investigations can be slow because of understaffing. DODIG has taken action on this issue, increasing the staffing of its whistleblower reprisal directorate from 17 staff in fiscal year 2006 to 30 staff in fiscal year 2011 to accommodate the increased caseload. In January 2012, DOD's Acting Inspector General authorized a further increase of staff for its whistleblower reprisal directorate from 30 to 42 (see fig. 3 for staffing at DODIG from fiscal years 2006 through 2011). Some service IG officials also indicated that staffing shortages are a factor in their ability to process cases in a timely manner.

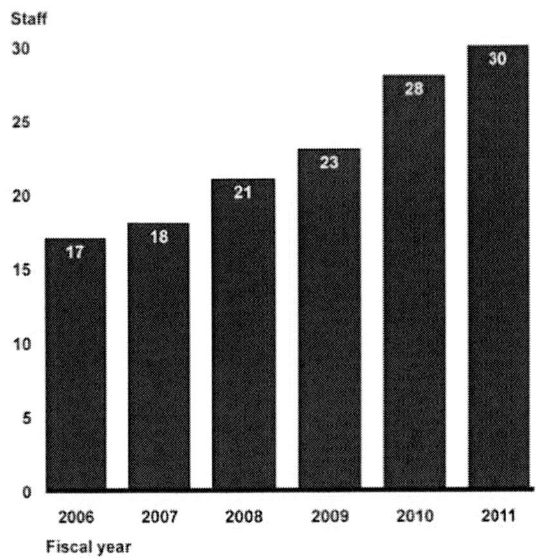

Source: GAO analysis of DODIG data.

Note: According to DODIG officials, the directorate responsible for investigating military whistleblower reprisals also had two detailees assigned to it in fiscal year 2009.

Figure 3. Average Number of Staff at the DODIG Military Whistleblower Reprisal Directorate from Fiscal Year 2006 through Fiscal Year 2011.

In a December 2011 letter, the DOD Inspector General asked the secretaries of the military departments to consider favorably any requests from the service IGs to increase their staffing in order to deal with the increased number of whistleblower reprisal cases.

DODIG has also undertaken multiple efforts to reform its investigative process to improve timeliness. For example, in late 2010, DODIG eliminated an investigative phase which required formal reports that recommended whether or not a case should be fully investigated. Earlier that year, DODIG eliminated the committee charged with reviewing and approving whether cases should be fully investigated. DODIG also changed its process for taking in complaints. The Defense Hotline[26] used to document the original complaint, gather additional information from complainants, and send it to the directorate at DODIG responsible for military whistleblower reprisal investigations. The Defense Hotline also was responsible for communicating with complainants if their cases were determined not to be whistleblower reprisal cases. Now the Defense Hotline passes the reprisal allegation to the directorate at DODIG responsible for military whistleblower reprisal investigations and investigators from that directorate establish direct contact with the complainant to assess the validity of the reprisal allegation(s). DODIG officials stated this new intake process is faster and increases the quality of the investigations because experienced reprisal investigators are in charge of information gathering. DODIG also started testing a new approach in evidence gathering to determine whether it can close cases more quickly.[27]

In contrast, the service IGs' processes for investigating these cases have generally remained the same. One major exception is the way Army cases are initially assessed. In order to deal with a large backlog in Army cases, DODIG and the Army IG signed a Memorandum of Agreement in 2008 whereby DODIG took over responsibility for conducting the initial review of all incoming Army complaints. The Memorandum of Agreement allowed the Army to focus on investigations and thereby reduce the Army's backlog of cases. Army and DODIG officials stated that this agreement was successful in reducing the Army's case backlog and improving case processing time.[28] Yet DODIG formally notified the Army IG in November 2011 that it would terminate this special arrangement as of May 2012. DODIG officials told us that they did so in order to maintain a consistent approach among the services and because the arrangement had increased DODIG's workload. In addition, they told us that cancelling the arrangement would enable their staff to conduct more full investigations. In November 2011, the Army IG asked DODIG to reconsider this decision, stating that the timeliness of Army reprisal investigations would suffer.[29] However, in December 2011, DODIG affirmed its decision to end the agreement with the Army.

Although DODIG has undertaken these and other efforts to improve its timeliness, it has generally not been completing investigations within the 180-day time frame provided by law. From our analysis of a random sample of 91 cases closed between January 1, 2009 through March 31, 2011, we estimate that 70 percent of the cases were not completed within 180 days; moreover, we estimated that it took DOD a mean of 451 days (+/- 94 days) to process the cases. Our random sample included a subset of 61 inquiries closed before full investigation, which took a mean of 469 days to close, and a subset of 28 full investigations, which took a mean of 395 days to close. 30,31 See table 3 for case processing time according to investigative phase.

Table 3. Mean Case Processing Time by Investigative Phase of Sampled Cases Closed between January 1, 2009 and March 31, 2011

Investigative phase	Number assessed	Total days (mean)	Percentage of cases over 180 days
All cases	91	451 *(+/- 94 days)*	70% *(+/- 11%)*
Cases closed before full investigation	61	469	64% *(39 of 61 cases)*
Full investigation	28	395	82% *(23 of 28 cases)*

☐ Data generalizable

▒ Data not generalizable

Source: GAO review of military whistleblower reprisal case files maintained by DODIG.

Notes:

Our random sample of 91 cases (out of a total of 871 cases closed during this time period) included 61 inquiries closed before full investigation and 28 cases closed after a full investigation. We were unable to determine the investigative phase in which 2 cases were closed.

Although data from the full sample are representative within the given parameters, any subset of these data cannot be assumed to be representative. That is, data specific to the cases closed before full investigation and the data specific to full investigation are not generalizable and apply only to the actual cases reviewed.

In addition to not completing investigations in 180 days in most cases, DOD has not complied with the statutory reporting requirement to provide notification in those instances where the investigations go beyond 180 days, although it is taking steps to do so.[32] The Military Whistleblower Protection Act requires the IG investigating an allegation of reprisal to submit to the Secretary of Defense and the complainant a notice if it cannot provide a report on the completed investigation within 180 days of the date the allegation was made to an IG in DOD. The notice should include the reason for the delay and an expected completion date for the investigation.33 DODIG officials acknowledged that they and the services had not been making the required notifications. The officials stated they used to submit these reports to the Secretary of Defense, but stopped doing so at some point because they were told by officials at the office receiving the notifications that they did not know what to do with the information.34 Because this notification is not being provided, as required by statute, the Secretary of Defense has had reduced visibility of cases that exceed the investigative time limit, and complainants have not been receiving information regarding their cases to which the law entitles them. During the course of our review, DODIG changed its practice and started reporting this information in October 2011. According to its October 2011 action plan, DODIG is taking steps to ensure that it and the service IGs follow the statutory reporting requirements.

DOD Efforts to Improve Case Processing Times Have Been Hindered by Unreliable and Incomplete Data

Although DOD has taken some steps to improve the timeliness of investigations, its efforts are hampered because DODIG does not have key timeliness data that would allow it to identify process areas requiring improvement or evaluate the impact of reforms. According to the quality standards for investigations, developed by the Council of the Inspectors General on Integrity and Efficiency, organizations should store data in a manner that allows for effective retrieval, referencing, and analysis. This enhances an organization's ability to conduct pattern and trend analyses and assists in the process of making informed judgments on investigative program development, and in the implementation of the investigative process.[35] Further, our prior work has shown that tracking timeliness is important for accountability and for making improvements to investigative processes.[36]

In our assessment of its data, we found that DODIG has not consistently or accurately recorded key dates to track how long investigations take to complete. From our analysis of a random sample of cases closed between January 1, 2009 through March 31, 2011, we estimate that DODIG's database understated the amount of days it took to close cases by a mean of 193 days (+/-76 days).[37] The understated number of days was a result of DODIG officials recording the date that they received a complaint in their office rather than the original date the complainant made the allegation to an IG in DOD. In addition, our case file review found that DODIG identified three cases as closed in its database when it actually referred these cases to a service for further investigation, resulting in an understatement of the amount of time it took to close cases. In one of these three cases, it took an additional 872 days to close the case. Moreover, our case file review found that 7 full investigations out of 28 had correct dates recorded in DODIG's database.[38] Table 4 provides timeliness accuracy by investigative phase.

Table 4. Timeliness Accuracy by Investigative Phase of Sampled Cases Closed between January 1, 2009 and March 31, 2011

Case type	Number assessed	Mean amount of days (DODIG database)	Actual mean amount of days (case file review)	Cases with accurately recorded dates in DODIG database
All cases	91	258 *(+/- 93 days)*	451 *(+/- 94 days)*	33% *(+/- 11%)*
Cases closed before full investigation	61	271	469	38% *(23 of 61 cases)*
Full investigation	28	242	395	25% *(7 of 28 cases)*

☐ Data generalizable

▒ Data not generalizable

Source: GAO review of military whistleblower reprisal case files maintained by DODIG.

Notes:

Our random sample of 91 cases (out of a total of 871 cases closed during this time period) included 61 inquiries closed before full investigation and 28 cases closed after a full investigation. We were unable to determine the investigative phase in which 2 cases were closed.

Although data from the full sample are representative within the given parameters, any subset of these data cannot be assumed to be representative. That is, data specific to the cases closed before full investigation and the data specific to full investigation are not generalizable and apply only to the actual cases reviewed.

DODIG's data practices have inhibited its ability to accurately identify the age of cases and therefore also prevented it from identifying cases in danger of exceeding the 180 days provided for investigations by the Military

Whistleblower Protection Act. DODIG has acknowledged it has problems with data reliability, calling the integrity of its data "questionable at best" in its October 2011 action plan for reforming the military whistleblower reprisal program. Further, during the course of our review, DODIG officials acknowledged that some of their dates for tracking cases were inaccurate. DODIG changed its approach starting in fiscal year 2012 so it now accurately records total case processing time. DODIG officials said they also planned to train investigators to ensure they consistently enter this information into DODIG's database.

In addition, DODIG has not been tracking the time the separate phases of the investigative process take. We found that the DODIG database includes fields for tracking dates by phases in the process. For example, there are date fields for referring cases to services for investigation and date fields for receiving those investigations from the services, but these were generally not filled out. Further, DODIG was not tracking the amount of time between when a complaint was filed with the Defense Hotline to when it was assigned to an investigator. We have previously found that comprehensive information is needed to identify reasons for delays in investigative processes.[39] DODIG officials acknowledged they can track timeliness data by process phases using their current systems and that doing so would enable them to understand the entire life cycle of military whistleblower reprisal investigations. Without identifying, collecting, and tracking accurate data, DODIG does not have reliable information to identify the scope of the challenge it faces with overall timeliness and cannot report accurate data to internal and external stakeholders, including data it reports in its semiannual reports to Congress. Moreover, DODIG may be unable to identify possible areas in the investigative process needing improvement, or assess the impact on timeliness of recent changes made to its process or of other actions taken to improve timeliness. During the course of our review, DODIG developed a plan to improve its practices associated with collecting and tracking timeliness information, including identifying date fields it should track, and training investigators to consistently enter this information. DODIG began to initiate these improvements starting in fiscal year 2012.

Congressional oversight of DODIG's ongoing efforts to improve data collection and management is hindered by the lack of available timeliness data. According to the *Standards for Internal Control in the Federal Government*, managers should provide reliable, useful, and timely information for accountability of government programs and their operations.[40] Although oversight is important for accountability, the IGs are intended to be independent and objective units, according to the Inspector General Act of 1978. Under the act, DODIG is not subject to regular organizational oversight inside DOD.[41] As a result, the Office of the Under Secretary of Defense for Personnel and Readiness—the organization designated by directive to receive notifications regarding reprisal investigations that exceed the 180-day time period, on behalf of the Secretary of Defense[42]—cannot provide organizational oversight of DODIG.[43]

DODIG officials stated that, although other offices within DOD cannot provide this type of oversight, the reporting requirement acts as a helpful internal check for DODIG on its timeliness progress. Congress is therefore the primary oversight body for DODIG. DODIG is required to keep Congress fully and currently informed through, among other things, its semiannual reports to Congress.

That report is required to include information on fraud, abuses, and deficiencies relating to the administration of programs and operations managed or financed by DOD.[44]

DODIG has not previously interpreted this requirement as applying to the military whistleblower reprisal program and does not provide information on military whistleblower reprisal case processing time, including the proportion of cases that exceed the 180-day time period provided by law, in the semiannual reports.

However, the absence of timeliness information in these reports limits congressional decision makers' ability to thoroughly evaluate and identify whether delays continue to exist within DOD's whistleblower reprisal investigative process.

As a result, Congress lacks information it could use to provide oversight of the military whistleblower reprisal program.

DODIG IS TAKING STEPS TO ADDRESS WHISTLEBLOWER REPRISAL PROCESS WEAKNESSES BUT OVERSIGHT CHALLENGES REMAIN

In an effort to improve its whistleblower program, DODIG has taken steps such as responding to the 2009 Department of Justice IG recommendations, completing an internal review, restructuring the organization primarily responsible for providing program oversight, and developing a plan of action. However, DODIG's oversight of this program still faces challenges because of the lack of performance metrics, outdated and inconsistently followed guidance, and the lack of standard monitoring processes and procedures for investigative cases.

DODIG Is Taking Steps to Address External and Internal Recommended Actions

DODIG has taken steps to improve the whistleblower reprisal process, including acting on prior recommendations. The 2009 Department of Justice report highlighted weaknesses in the military whistleblower program and made recommendations for improvements such as creating and updating written policy guidance regarding whistleblower law.[45] DODIG conducted an internal review, completed in 2011, to assess the progress it had made since beginning to take actions to address the findings of the Department of Justice report.[46] This report made additional recommendations to help improve DODIG's oversight of the whistleblower reprisal program, including that DODIG conduct an internal audit of its case tracking system to help ensure timely case processing.

In October 2011, DODIG developed an action plan that outlined its strategy to address the program weaknesses identified in the 2009 Department of Justice report and its 2011 internal review, and has begun to implement that strategy. We have already mentioned some of the changes DODIG is undertaking based on the action plan, including changes to the report review processes. As part of the reform plan, DODIG restructured its directorate in charge of military whistleblower reprisal investigations in October 2011, merging it with the directorate responsible for civilian whistleblower reprisal investigations. One of the goals of this merger is to increase the consistency of reprisal investigations within DOD. Additionally, the merger is intended to eventually create a pool of investigators that can work on both military and civilian reprisal cases, thereby maximizing DODIG's flexibility to adjust to spikes in reprisal cases and clear any case backlogs. The immediate past DOD Inspector General also told us that one of the most significant changes he made was putting a robust new leadership team in place dedicated to improving the military whistleblower reprisal program and transforming it into a model program.

DODIG has also revised its case intake process as part of its reform efforts. Reprisal allegations that are made directly to DODIG rather than a service can come in through the Defense Hotline over the phone or using an automated web-based form. DODIG has made multiple changes in the last several years to its process for taking in and initially assessing if these cases qualify as reprisal cases. The 2011 internal review found that DODIG's intake process was still requiring complainants to provide a significant amount of documentary evidence to support their reprisal allegations. The internal review concluded the emphasis on documentation at this very early stage just to determine if the allegations warranted investigation was inconsistent with the basic information required when filing complaints with the Defense Hotline. Further, the internal review found that the documentation demands required at this stage could produce an onerous burden for the complainant and were inconsistent with DODIG guidance. In response, DODIG is instituting changes to quickly assign an investigator to a case, who then makes direct contact with the complainant and initiates an investigation based on the standard that, "the alleged fact, if true, would raise the inference of reprisal."

DOD's Implementation of Oversight Mechanisms Is Not Yet Complete and Faces Challenges

Although DODIG has taken steps to improve its military whistleblower reprisal program, its ability to provide oversight continues to face key challenges due to the lack of performance metrics, outdated and inconsistently followed guidance, and inconsistent monitoring processes and procedures to track all reprisal allegations. According to Standards for Internal Control in the Federal Government, oversight mechanisms are an integral part of an entity's planning, implementing, reviewing, and of the accountability for stewardship of government resources and achieving effective results.[47] Oversight mechanisms include, among other things, the written policies, procedures, techniques, performance measures, and mechanisms that enforce management's directives and help ensure that actions can be taken to address risks. While DOD's action plan offers many important steps towards achieving a model whistleblower reprisal program, these actions are ongoing, and to date have not been fully implemented.

Performance Metrics

DODIG has not yet fully established performance metrics for whistleblower investigations although it is taking steps to do so. Federal internal control standards say metrics are important for identifying and setting appropriate incentives for achieving goals while complying with law, regulations, and ethical standards.[48] DODIG officials recognize the importance of metrics and have told us that they are currently working to create timeliness metrics that focus on case processing time. However, they have not yet formalized these metrics. We have previously found that timeliness alone does not provide a complete picture of an investigative process and that metrics on quality, such as completeness of investigative reports and the adequacy of internal controls, enhance the ability of organizations to provide assurance that it is exercising all of the appropriate safeguards for federal programs.[49] Further, measuring timeliness alone may provide incentive to close cases prematurely.[50] For example, DODIG could theoretically close and report on all cases before they reach 180 days in order to meet the timeliness standard. However, meeting that standard alone would not ensure that cases were properly investigated. DODIG currently lacks metrics to measure quality, but DODIG officials recognize that metrics on quality are important and indicated that they plan to develop them as part of their effort to improve case management and outcomes. The officials said that such metrics could include measuring whether interviews are completed and documented and whether conclusions made about the case are fully supported by evidence.

Our review of case files revealed that documents that could be used to support the conclusions of a case were not always present in DODIG's case files. For example, according to DODIG's investigations manual,[51] every case file should have some sort of documented investigative analysis that lays out the evidence and conclusions the evidence supports. The level of investigative analysis we looked for in each case file depended on how far the case proceeded. For cases that were closed in the very early stages of the investigation, an oversight worksheet summarizing the reasons for closing a case was sufficient for the purpose of our file review. For cases that went to full investigation, we looked for a formal record of investigation. We found evidence of investigative analysis in 79 (87 percent) of the 91 case files. Additionally, DODIG requires that investigations that go beyond the initial review include a record of testimony from the complainant. Full investigations are also required to include a record of an interview with the subject. When reviewing the cases for this document, we found evidence of a record of testimony in 38 (49 percent) of the 77 cases that required it. Although we looked in our case file review for the types of documents that would support DODIG's conclusions, we did not determine whether the evidence in each file actually supported DODIG's conclusions for each case. However, an internal DODIG review found that some cases DODIG adjudicated contained insufficient documentation to support the findings or evidence that necessary investigative steps were completed. The internal review team further noted that they did not disagree with the final outcomes of the cases, only that they could not affirm the decisions because the information in some of the file did not support it. Without clear quality metrics, DODIG will continue to lack valuable information it could use to improve oversight of the whistleblower reprisal investigative process.

Guidance

Although DODIG is updating its outdated guidance related to the whistleblower program, the updates have not yet been formalized and the existing guidance is inconsistently followed. According to the framework set out in quality standards for investigations, organizations should establish appropriate written investigative policies and procedures through handbook, manual, directives, or similar mechanism to facilitate due professional care in meeting program requirements.52 Further, that guidance should be regularly evaluated to ensure that it is still appropriate and working as intended. DODIG has guidance regarding the whistleblower reprisal process in place but has not updated it to reflect changes in its investigative practices or ensured that certain provisions have been carried out consistently. For example, DODIG's primary investigative guide distributed to investigators conducting whistleblower reprisal investigations has not been updated since 1996 and does not reflect some current investigative practices.53 The investigative guide directs investigators to appendices that no longer exist and states that whistleblower reprisal investigation reports must be completed and issued within 90 days of the receipt of the allegation instead of the 180 days provided under the statute as amended in 1998. Officials from the service IGs told us that the old guidance still provides them with some benefit regarding general investigative approaches but said that it would be beneficial to them if it was updated. Additionally, DODIG officials acknowledge that the current guidance reflects old investigative approaches that have since been revised, such as the investigator checklist, or that no longer exist. The lack of updated guidance has been a recurring issue for DODIG. A 2002 DODIG briefing stated that the investigative guide required updating and that the update was nearing completion. The 2009 Department of Justice IG report also found that guidance for service IGs had not been adequate and that DODIG could improve oversight of service IG work by creating and updating written policy guidance regarding whistleblower law, including recurring and emerging issues, best practices, and precedent. Moreover, the 2011 internal review came to a similar conclusion and recommended that DODIG update the investigative guides to ensure consistency and objectivity in processing cases. DODIG indicated that it planned to revise its investigative guidance in both its response to the Department of Justice report as well as in its response to the 2011 internal review. DODIG officials told us that they are working with internal stakeholders to revise the guidance to reflect current practices and plan on updating the 1996 investigative by the third quarter of fiscal year 2012. Without updated guidance on investigations, DODIG does not have a documented consistent investigative standard for its whistleblower program.

In addition to being outdated, DODIG's existing guidance related to the whistleblower program is not consistently followed. We have reported that program guidance should be regularly evaluated to ensure that it is still appropriate and working as intended.[54] The guidance related to certain key provisions of the investigative process is unclear, leading to inconsistent implementation among the service IGs. For example, the service IGs have adopted different interpretations of the 180-day reporting requirement as it is set out in the guidance. As noted earlier in the report, the Military Whistleblower Protection Act requires that IGs conducting investigations issue a report of investigation to the complainant and the Secretary of Defense within 180 days of the receipt of an allegation or provide appropriate notice if unable to do so. The law also requires DODIG to approve the report of investigation before the report is issued. Further, officials from DODIG and the service IGs emphasized that whistleblower reprisal cases are not closed until DODIG has reviewed the complaint and the evidence to support the investigators' conclusions and formally agrees with the disposition of the case. However, DOD Directive 7050.06 sets out additional time frames for reporting. The directive requires the service IGs to provide DODIG with a report of investigation within 180 days of receiving the complaint or receiving a request for an investigation from DODIG and requires them to provide a report of investigation to the complainant and the Secretary of Defense not later than 30 days after the DODIG approves the report. A service IG could meet the first requirement but at the same time leave no time for DODIG to review and approve the report in time to issue it within the 180 days provided by law.[55] As a result, the service IGs have adopted different interpretations of the directive's 180-day reporting requirement. For example, Air Force IG officials told us that the Air Force recently reinterpreted the reporting requirement. The Air Force had set an internal goal of completing reprisal investigation within 135 days to allow 45 days for DODIG review and approval. However, the Air Force told us that it now sets its internal investigation deadline to 180 days and therefore no longer accounts for DODIG review time. The Army IG stated that it had the same interpretation of the 180-day reporting requirement as the Air Force IG. Officials from the Navy and Marine Corps IGs told us they generally include DODIG review in their interpretation of the 180-day reporting requirement. DODIG officials are aware of some of the different interpretations among the services and the conflicts that exist in the current directive. According to DODIG, it will be sending written guidance to the services to reemphasize that the 180-day statutory time frame is prescribed as from the time the complaint is filed until the time the report is submitted to the complainant. DODIG reported that it will also incorporate the clarifying language into the directive and will begin the process of revising DOD Directive 7050.06 in the second quarter of 2012.

DODIG also has not been consistently adhering to standards regarding the maintenance of its case files and, as a result, its case files are generally incomplete. Quality Standards for Investigations outline standards related to case file management and state that the file folders used to document an investigation should be accurate and complete, and the investigative report findings and accomplishments must be supported by adequate documentation and maintained in the case file.[56] According to DODIG's standards related to the management of these files, it is important for case files to adequately represent the investigative work and evidence underlying the conclusions and recommendations in the final report, and to be thoroughly documented to ensure that the files will be able to withstand scrutiny.[57] Based on a review of DODIG's process, relevant statutes, directives, and other standards, and in consultation with DODIG officials, we identified 18 key elements that we believe should be present in case files to provide support for conclusions, document compliance with the law or directives, or help manage the case. Using our sample of 91 cases, we assessed the presence of the key elements as indicators of the completeness of the file.[58] Based on the presence in the file of the elements we selected, we found that most of DODIG's case files were incomplete (56 percent) or partially complete (38 percent) and only a small portion of the case files were complete (5 percent). See table 5 for further details.

We also found that the guidance regarding a key investigative question is unclear. According to DODIG's investigative guide,[59] an investigation is complete when the four questions of the "Acid Test" have been answered (see fig. 2). We estimate that 65 percent of the cases closed between January 1, 2009 and March 31, 2011, were closed, at least in part, because DODIG concluded that the personnel action would have occurred even if the protected communication had not been made— question 4 of the Acid Test (see app. II for further details on the reasons DODIG closed cases). The departmental guidance for addressing all four questions instructs the investigator to investigate the complaint, and not the complainant, noting that investigators should avoid the tendency to examine the reputation, background, or performance of the complainant in order to determine the credibility of the complainant's claim. However, in answering the fourth question, the guidance requires, among other things, an examination of the reasonableness of the unfavorable personnel action(s) taken, withheld, or threatened considering the complainant's performance and conduct. DODIG officials acknowledged that there may be some tension between these two requirements.

Table 5. Estimated Level of DODIG Case File Folder Completeness for Cases Closed between January 1, 2009 and March 31, 2011

Level of case file completeness	Number of cases (out of 91)	Percentage of cases
Complete[a]	5	5% (+/-11%)
Partially complete[b]	35	38% (+/-11%)
Incomplete[c]	51	56% (+/-11%)

Source: GAO analysis of DOD information.

Notes:

Based on a review of 91 files of the original random sample of 97 for cases closed between January 1, 2009 and March 31, 2011.

Percentages do not add up to 100 percent due to rounding.

We identified 18 elements and used those as indicators for the completeness of a file. However, not all 18 elements needed to be present in every file. For example, some of the 18 elements would only need to be present in a file if an investigation was conducted by a service, went beyond 180 days, or was a full investigation. We adjusted the required number of elements based on the specific circumstances of each case and calculated completeness based on that adjusted baseline. See app. I for further details on the scope and methodology.

[a] We assessed a case file to be complete if it contained 85 percent or more of the documents that should be present.

[b] We assessed a case file to be partially complete if it contained between 70 and 84 percent of the documents that should be present.

[c] We assessed a case file to be incomplete if it contained less than 70 percent of the documents that should be present.

Further, in its October 2011 action plan, DODIG stated that current guidance for question 4 has resulted in investigators closing cases prematurely without fully considering whether the subject's actions are consistent with actions taken in similar situations with other employees.

As a result, DODIG officials are revising guidance for the investigative questions. However, until DODIG carries out these actions, the lack of clear guidance hinders efforts to ensure consistent program implementation.

Case Monitoring Processes and Procedures

DODIG officials acknowledge the importance of standard case monitoring processes and procedures, but currently lack such processes and procedures, which may hinder their ability to consistently assess the status of outstanding reprisal cases. According to federal internal control standards, monitoring of internal controls should be conducted to assess the quality of performance over time.[60] DODIG has responsibility for not only conducting its own investigations, but also for overseeing and approving the investigations conducted by service and other component IGs.[61] It can be challenging for DODIG to maintain visibility on all cases because a reprisal allegation can be made to and investigated by one of several IGs in DOD.

DODIG has not established standard monitoring processes and procedures and instead has been relying on ad hoc and inconsistent efforts. For example, some service IG officials told us that they had not reconciled cases with the DODIG in several years and some service IG officials have recently been queried about cases that date back 5 years. DODIG and service officials told us that DODIG had not required service IGs to regularly report on the status of open cases. Additionally, our file review included a case where the DODIG identified an investigation begun by a service IG 6 years prior but never closed. DODIG was unable to establish contact with the complainant after 6 years and later administratively closed the case. Although this could be an extreme case, it may be indicative of a larger issue dealing with the tracking and management of complaints. Further, DODIG officials told us that the review of whistleblower reprisal cases involving senior level officials had in the past been handled by another office within DODIG and that the whistleblower reprisal directorate had limited visibility on the status of these cases. However, according to DODIG, it changed this procedure in late fiscal year 2011 so that the directorate responsible for whistleblower reprisal investigations also investigates or oversees service reprisal investigations involving senior officials. Moreover, DODIG's action plan outlines its approach to providing more consistent monitoring of all reprisal cases, including investigations of senior officials that include reprisal allegations. The first step in this plan has been to establish a team of investigators dedicated to providing oversight of service investigations. DODIG officials told us that once this team has worked through the backlog of cases, it will also implement more efforts to consistently monitor and reconcile cases to help ensure that all reprisal allegations are appropriately addressed in a timely manner. Until it further addresses the weaknesses in its monitoring practices of military whistleblower reprisal cases and the challenges it faces in its other oversight mechanisms, DODIG cannot be sure that it is adequately conducting its oversight responsibilities or implementing the whistleblower reprisal program as intended.

DOD Efforts to Ensure Corrective Actions Are Taken in Substantiated Cases Are Hindered by Disconnected Investigative and Corrective Action Processes and Unreliable Data

DOD's efforts to ensure that appropriate corrective action is taken after investigations are completed—both for whistleblowers and against those who reprise against whistleblowers—are hampered by disconnected investigative and corrective action processes and the limited visibility of corrective actions taken. Individuals with substantiated military whistleblower reprisal cases generally receive relief from the negative impacts caused by reprisal when they seek it from the BCMRs (80 percent of those who apply). However, few individuals with substantiated cases apply to the BCMRs for relief (19.1 percent). DODIG and the service BCMRs are also not consistently identifying and tracking data on corrective action taken to undo the damage done to the complainant by the reprisal. Further, unreliable data regarding corrective action taken against the subject are hindering oversight of this key aspect of whistleblower protection.

Few Servicemembers with Substantiated Cases Apply for the Relief Process

Most servicemembers with substantiated cases who seek relief from BCMRs receive it, but few apply for relief and so the secretaries of the military departments and the heads of the other DOD components are not generally able to take action to make the complainant whole in the vast majority of cases. The DOD directive governing the military whistleblower reprisal process, DOD Directive 7050.06, includes a largely service-centered process for obtaining corrective action that is separate from the investigative process centered on DODIG. Specifically, the directive charges the secretaries of the military departments and the heads of the other DOD components with taking corrective action based on the IG investigation.[62] Corrective action includes: (1) any action deemed necessary to make the complainant whole, (2) changes in agency regulations or practices, (3) administrative or disciplinary action against offending personnel, or (4) referral to the U.S. Attorney General or court-martial convening authority of any evidence of criminal violation. Although DODIG can investigate allegations of reprisal, makes all final determinations on investigations, and can make recommendations regarding appropriate corrective action, it does not have the authority to take corrective action, either for the complainant or against the subject. In order for servicemembers to receive relief from the negative impacts caused by reprisal—even for cases substantiated by DODIG—the law requires that servicemembers must file a separate application to their service BCMR.[63] For cases that are substantiated and those that are not, DODIG provides the appropriate service BCMR with the same case outcome notification it provides to the complainant. However, the DODIG notification letter does not automatically trigger a BCMR review of the case and/or corrective action.

For cases that servicemembers bring to the BCMRs, the Military Whistleblower Protection Act requires the BCMRs to review the whistleblower reprisal report approved by DODIG. However, BCMRs have authority to make independent determinations on military whistleblower reprisal cases and to engage in additional fact finding. Among other things, the statute also allows the BCMRs to request that DODIG or the service IGs gather additional evidence for the BCMR's consideration and hold hearings, although BCMR and DODIG officials told us that, to their knowledge, this authority had not ever been exercised. Further, it is up to the BCMR to make its own determination whether personnel action was in reprisal and recommend to the secretary of the military department appropriate actions to correct the record of those who have been reprised against. However, BCMR officials told us that they put significant credence in DODIG's findings and that their offices place a high priority on military whistleblower reprisal cases even though they make up only a small proportion of their total work.[64]

Table 6. Substantiated Reprisal Cases Submitted to BCMRs and Their Outcome for Cases Closed between Fiscal Year 2006 and the First Half of Fiscal Year 2011

BCMR	Cases submitted to BCMR by complainant	Cases where BCMR provided a remedy	Remedy provided (percent)
Air Force	9	9	100%
Army	6	3	50%
Navy (all)[a]	10	8	80%
Navy[a]	9	8	89%
Marine Corps[a]	1	0	—
Total	**25**	**20**	**80%**

Source: GAO analysis of DOD information.

Notes:

Based on DODIG data for cases that included military whistleblower reprisal allegations substantiated by DODIG between October 1, 2005 and March 31, 2011, and BCMR data regarding the cases submitted to them, including case outcome.

Data do not include cases in which, according to DODIG data, the military whistleblower reprisal allegations were not substantiated but an improper referral for mental health evaluation (IMHE) was substantiated. Including those figures boosts the total number of cases submitted to the BCMRs to 31 and boosts the number of cases where the BCMR provided a remedy to 25, or 81 percent.

The Navy BCMR reviews cases for the Department of the Navy and therefore handles cases from both Navy personnel and Marine Corps personnel.

Two cases (one Army, one Marine Corps) in which a complainant submitted an application to a BCMR were not included because the BCMRs had not yet completed action on them.

Remedy provided indicates that the complainant received at least partial remedy. It does not indicate that the complainants received the exact remedy they were seeking.

[a]Two Navy BCMR cases—one from the Marine Corps and one from the Navy—were included and considered as not having received remedy although the Navy BCMR data are unclear whether or not it provided remedy. If the Navy BCMR provided remedy in these cases, then all Navy and Marine Corps substantiated whistleblower reprisal allegations brought before the BCMR received some remedy.

In our review of all substantiated reprisal cases submitted to BCMRs between fiscal year 2006 and the first half of fiscal year 2011, we found that the servicemembers with substantiated whistleblower reprisal allegations that applied for relief were generally successful in obtaining some relief.[65] Eighty percent of servicemembers (20 of 25) with substantiated reprisal cases—closed between fiscal year 2006 through the first half of 2011—who sought relief from a BCMR received some sort of remedy (see table 6).

The most common corrective action taken by the services in response to applications filed by complainants with substantiated military whistleblower reprisal allegations was amending or removing a rating from the complainant's personnel record. This occurred in 14 of the 25 substantiated cases brought to the BCMRs.

For example, in 1of the cases a servicemember with a substantiated whistleblower reprisal case requested that the Army BCMR remove two ratings from his record.

The Army BCMR decided to remove the one rating that the DODIG found was done in reprisal. The second most common corrective action taken by the services was providing payment, benefits, awards, or training that was denied as a result of the reprisal.

This occurred in 6 of the 25 substantiated cases brought to the BCMRs. For example, in one of the cases, a servicemember was given a Bronze Star that had been denied to him because of a reprisal. The third most common corrective action taken by the services was amending or removing disciplinary actions from an individual's personnel record. For example, the Air Force BCMR removed a letter of reprimand from a servicemember's file that DODIG found was a result of an act of reprisal. This occurred in 4 of the 25 substantiated cases brought to the BCMRs. There were also a number of cases where the service took more than one corrective action. For example, a Navy petty officer had a disciplinary action removed from his record, a promotion backdated, and retroactive pay instated to go along with the backdated promotion.

Although 80 percent of servicemembers with substantiated whistleblower reprisal allegations who applied for relief received some relief, only about 1 in 5 servicemembers with whistleblower reprisal allegations substantiated by DODIG applied to the BCMRs for relief during the time period we reviewed. As shown in table 7, only 25 of the 131 (19.1 percent) of complainants with substantiated cases submitted applications for relief with their BCMR. As a result, only 15 percent of servicemembers with reprisal allegations substantiated by DODIG received some relief through their BCMRs.

Table 7. Substantiated Reprisal Cases Submitted to BCMRs Compared to All Substantiated Cases for Cases Closed Between Fiscal Year 2006 and the First Half of Fiscal Year 2011

BCMR	Total cases substantiated	Cases submitted to BCMR by complainant	Cases where BCMR provided a remedy	Percentage of total cases substantiated	
				Case submitted	Remedy provided
Air Force	58	9	9	15.5%	15.5%
Army	54	6	3	11.1%	5.6%
Navy (all)[a]	19	10	8	52.6%	42.1%
Navy[a]	17	9	8	52.9%	47.1%
Marine Corps[a]	2	1	0	50%	0
Total	131	25	20	19.1%	15.3%

Source: GAO analysis of DOD information.

Notes:

Based on DODIG data for cases that included military whistleblower reprisal allegations substantiated by DODIG between October 1, 2005 and March 31, 2011, and BCMR data regarding the cases submitted to them, including case outcome.

Total substantiated cases do not include two cases (one Army, one Marine Corps) in which a complainant submitted an application to a BCMR because the BCMRs had not yet completed action on them. It also does not include 2 Army cases that, according to data provided by the Army BCMR, DODIG misidentified in their database as containing substantiated whistleblower reprisal claims when they had substantiated only improper referral for mental health evaluations (IMHE).

Data does not include cases in which, according to DODIG data, the military whistleblower reprisal allegations are not substantiated but an improper referral for mental health evaluation (IMHE) is substantiated. Including those figures does not significantly impact total cases submitted—the percent changes from 19.1 percent to 19.0 percent. Total remedy provided is 15.3 percent in both cases.

The Navy BCMR reviews cases for the Department of the Navy and therefore handles cases from both Navy personnel and Marine Corps personnel.

There were 9 cases in which complainants did not apply to the Army BCMR for record correction where the BCMR could not have provided relief had the complainant applied. The BCMR could not have provided relief because the substantiated claim did not impact the complainant's record. For example, the complainant was threatened with adverse action or was restricted from making a lawful communication to an IG or Member of Congress. Neither action would result in a negative impact on the complainant's personnel file. Not counting these Army cases would change the Army cases submitted and Army remedy provided to 13.3 percent and 6.7 percent, respectively. It would also change the total cases submitted and total remedy provided to 20.5 percent and 16.4 percent, respectively.

We did not identify similar circumstances for cases processed by the Air Force and Navy BCMRs based on the information provided by these organizations.\

Remedy provided indicates that complainants received at least partial remedy. It does not indicate that complainants received the exact remedy they were seeking.

[a]Two Navy BCMR cases—one from the Marine Corps and one from the Navy—were included and considered as not having received remedy, although the Navy BCMR data are unclear whether or not it provided remedy. If the Navy BCMR provided remedy in these cases, then all Navy and Marine Corps substantiated whistleblower reprisal allegations brought before the BCMR received some remedy.

We found that there were differences between the services regarding the proportion of cases submitted to the BCMRs, with more than half of the substantiated Navy cases being brought to the Navy BCMR and only approximately 1 in 10 substantiated Army cases being brought to the Army BCMR.

Officials from DODIG, the service IGs, and the BCMRs indicated that they did not know the exact reason why so few servicemembers with substantiated reprisal allegations apply for relief. There are some cases for which the BCMRs cannot provide relief. For example, a BCMR cannot correct the record for an individual where DODIG substantiated that the individual was threatened with reprisal but where no actual harm was done to that individual's record. Similarly, a BCMR cannot correct the record for an individual where DODIG substantiated that the individual was restricted from making a lawful communication to an IG in DOD or Member of Congress. We identified nine Army cases where the Army BCMR was not in a position to provide relief. Discounting those nine cases would increase the percentage of servicemembers with substantiated claims that submitted cases to the Army BCMR from 11.1 percent to 13.3 percent (see table 7 and associated notes for further details). However, the overall impact of such cases appears to be minimal due to the relatively low number of substantiated cases involving only restriction or threats of reprisal.[66] Officials from the Air Force and Army BCMRs also said that some servicemembers may be seeking relief from other lower-level service boards, such as the Air Force Evaluation Report Appeals Board or the Army's Enlisted Special Review Board, even though servicemembers are told in their letter from DODIG to obtain relief from the BCMRs. The officials did not know of any such incidents but said it was a possibility. Data obtained from the Army BCMR shows four such incidents, with the other board providing relief to the servicemember in one of the four cases. Discounting those four cases would increase the percentage of servicemembers with substantiated claims that submitted cases to the Army

BCMR from 11.1 percent to 12.0 percent.[67] Based on these data, the impact of complainants taking cases to boards other than BCMR is relatively modest and does not explain the large difference between the number of substantiated cases and the number of cases brought to the BCMRs.

Service and DODIG officials also stated that the length of time it takes for servicemembers to get their reprisal allegations substantiated may impact their willingness to engage in yet another process. Servicemembers frequently rotate to other assignments at different locations around the world and so could be in a completely new work environment with a different chain of command by the time the reprisal investigation is completed. The officials also said that servicemembers may have left the service during the time it takes to substantiate a claim. Our case file review included a nongeneralizable subset of seven substantiated whistleblower reprisal cases that took a mean of 614 days to close and with a range of 439 days to 796 days. Only one of the seven servicemembers with a substantiated case from our file review applied for relief with their BCMR, and DODIG took 750 days to substantiate that one claim.

A further factor that could impact the willingness of those with substantiated reprisal claims from pursuing remedy from their service BCMR is a lack of understanding regarding the available remedies. The Military Whistleblower Protection Act allows a report of investigation to include recommendations regarding the corrective action. According to DODIG's investigative guide, recommendations should be made if there is a substantiated reprisal allegation.

It states that recommendations can be general or specific but that the corrective action "should be sufficient to make the complainant 'whole' and restore the complainant to the same or equal status he or she would have attained if the reprisal had not occurred."

According to DODIG officials, DODIG used to provide detailed recommendations regarding what it thought would be appropriate remedies for the complainant. For example, the 1996 investigative guide includes an example of a case that recommends a specific evaluation report be voided and the complainant be reinstated to his former position or one commensurate to it. Nevertheless, DODIG's current practice is to provide a more general recommendation that appropriate corrective action be taken. DODIG officials did not know when or why this change in practice occurred but acknowledged that it would be appropriate and helpful to provide more detailed recommendations for how to make the complainant whole. Without knowing more about when and how this practice changed, we were not able to identify if there is an association between the level of detail in recommendations and the proportion of individuals who apply to the BCMRs.

However, it is reasonable to assume that without detailing in the investigative report the types of remedies that could be appropriate, the servicemember may not be aware of the full benefit realized by applying for relief to the BCMR.

Service BCMRs Are Not Consistently Identifying Reprisal Cases

The service BCMRs are not consistently identifying applicants who have substantiated reprisal cases as such and are therefore not providing all reprisal victims with the procedural privileges to which they are entitled. The Military Whistleblower Protection Act[68] provides whistleblowers with unique procedural privileges that are generally not afforded to other applicants to the BCMRs. These privileges include:

1. direct application for corrective action may be made to the service BCMR instead of first going to a lower level of administrative appeal;[69]
2. 180-day deadline for the BCMR to review and the secretary of the military department concerned to render a final decision in the case, which differs from other cases processed by BCMRs; and
3. right to appeal BCMR decisions to the Secretary of Defense.[70]

Further, according to federal internal control standards, agencies need operating information to determine whether they are achieving their compliance requirements under various laws and regulations.[71] BCMR officials also told us that whistleblower reprisal cases are high-priority cases for the BCMRs, even though they receive only a few a year compared to the many thousands of other cases they process. They therefore make a special effort to track reprisal cases.[72]

Although the Military Whistleblower Protection Act provides unique procedural privileges to whistleblowers who apply to BCMRs for relief, the BCMRs are not consistently identifying applicants with substantiated whistleblower reprisal cases as such and are therefore not always aware when these procedural privileges should apply.73 We found that the BCMRs did not identify 10 of the 25 applicants with whistleblower reprisal cases substantiated by DODIG as whistleblower reprisal cases (see table 8).

Table 8. Comparison of Substantiated Cases Identified and Not Identified as Reprisal by the BCMRs (for Cases Closed between Fiscal Year 2006 and the First Half of Fiscal Year 2011)

	All reprisal cases submitted to BCMR	Cases identified by BCMR reprisal	Cases not identified by BCMR as reprisal
Number of cases	25	15	10
Percent of all cases	100%	60%	40%
Mean days to close case	179	133	249
Cases over 180 days	9	4	5
Percent of cases over 180 days	36%	27%	50%
Remedy provided	20	12	8
Percent remedy provided	80%	80%	80%

Source: GAO analysis of DOD information.

Notes:

Based on DODIG data for cases that included military whistleblower reprisal allegations substantiated by DODIG between October 1, 2005 and March 31, 2011, and BCMR data regarding the cases submitted to them, including case outcome.

The Navy BCMR reviews cases for the Department of the Navy and therefore handles cases from both Navy personnel and Marine Corps personnel.

Two cases (one Army, one Marine Corps) in which a complainant submitted an application to a BCMR were not included because the BCMRs had not yet completed action on them.

Two Navy BCMR cases—one from the Marine Corps and one from the Navy—were included and considered as not having received remedy, although the Navy BCMR data are unclear whether or not it provided remedy. The Marine Corps case was not identified by the Navy BCMR as being a military whistleblower reprisal case. The Navy case was identified as a military whistleblower reprisal case.

A more detailed table by service can be found in app. III.

Remedy provided indicates that the complainant received at least partial remedy. It does not indicate that the complainant received the exact remedy they were seeking.

Additionally, we found in the aggregate that cases that are not identified as whistleblower reprisal cases took longer. This was true for each BCMR but was more pronounced with the Navy BCMR. Data provided by the Navy BCMR showed that it processed in 40 days (mean) the six cases that were identified as reprisal in their database but took 235 days (mean) to process four cases not identified as reprisal (see app. III). Between those cases identified as reprisal and those that were not, we did not observe a difference in overall proportion of applicants who were provided remedy by the BCMRs.

However, complainants who do not receive remedy or are not satisfied by the remedy they received from the BCMR and who the BCMR did not identify as a whistleblower reprisal case are not informed of their right to appeal to the Secretary of Defense. Instead, these individuals are treated as non-whistleblower applicants and so told that their administrative appeals options have been exhausted within the service, unless they have new information to provide to the BCMRs. The applicants are also advised that they may seek remedy in a court of appropriate jurisdiction.

We identified two factors that may impact the ability to consistently identify substantiated military whistleblower reprisal cases across all of the service BCMRs. First, service BCMR officials told us that they may not be properly identifying all whistleblower reprisal cases in their case tracking system because it is not always readily apparent on a complainant's application that it is a whistleblower case. The form used by whistleblowers to apply for relief from a BCMR is the same general form used by all applicants to the BCMRs. This form requires a narrative description and does not have a special indicator, such as a checkbox, to identify the case as a whistleblower reprisal case. The officials said that their intake organizations and reviewers could therefore miss that an applicant is a whistleblower if the applicant did not explicitly mention it.

Second, the different approaches service BCMRs take to DODIG notifications of substantiated cases they receive may also impact how consistently they identify military whistleblower reprisal cases. The success of identifying military whistleblower reprisal cases varies by service BCMR, with the Army properly identifying 83 percent of the cases (5 of 6), the Navy identifying 60 percent of the cases (6 of 10), and the Air Force identifying 44 percent of the cases (4 of 9) for cases closed between fiscal year 2006 and the first half of fiscal year 2011 (see app. III). Army BCMR officials told us that a method they used to identify military whistleblower reprisal cases is to create an electronic case file for every substantiated case notification they receive from DODIG. Although they immediately close the case in the database, it acts as a flag to identify a case as a whistleblower reprisal case should a complainant apply to the Army BCMR for relief. The Air Force and Navy BCMRs do not have a similar procedure. By not properly identifying a significant proportion of whistleblower reprisal cases as reprisal cases, the

BCMRs are not providing all whistleblower applicants with the unique procedural privileges afforded them by law.

Unreliable Data Limits Visibility and Oversight of Corrective Action

DODIG lacks reliable data on the corrective action taken in response to substantiated whistleblower reprisal cases, which limits the visibility and oversight DOD and Congress have of the final portion of the military whistleblower reprisal process. According to federal internal control standards, oversight mechanisms are an integral part of an entity's planning, implementing, reviewing, and accountability for stewardship of government resources and achieving effective results.[74] Oversight mechanisms include the policies, procedures, techniques, and mechanisms that enforce management's directives and help ensure that actions are taken to address risks. The impact of whistleblower reprisal investigations comes with the corrective actions taken in response to substantiated cases. Additionally, the 2009 Department of Justice review recommended that the results of investigations that substantiate allegations of reprisal be publicized as a way to heighten awareness within the services of the Military Whistleblower Protection Act, to potentially deter future incidents of reprisal, and to possibly encourage other reprisal victims to come forward.

While DODIG cannot directly take corrective action in response to a substantiated case, it is the focal point for DOD's military whistleblower reprisal program and is well positioned to collect and monitor data regarding program outcomes. DODIG has a directorate dedicated primarily to whistleblower reprisal allegation investigations and designated to receive information from the military departments on corrective action, so is well positioned not only to collect the information on corrective action but also to use that information to help enhance oversight of the military whistleblower reprisal process and ensure that it is achieving effective results. DODIG officials stated that because DODIG is the focal point for DOD's military whistleblower reprisal activities, it is important for them to have visibility and information of all military whistleblower reprisal activities, not only to provide oversight but also to provide a central place within the department where internal and external stakeholders can obtain information. They explained that they would want to know, for example, if complainants were having difficulty obtaining corrective action so that they could try to address such a problem.

They also noted that it was important to have complete data since Members of Congress come to DODIG for information on military whistleblower reprisal activities. The officials emphasized that understanding the relevance of their investigative work depends on knowing what corrective action was taken in response to that work.

Although DODIG officials acknowledge the importance of information on corrective action, the service BCMRs are not consistently reporting and DODIG is not maintaining data on the actions BCMRs take in response to reprisal cases. DOD Directive 7050.06 requires the secretaries of the military departments to notify DODIG and the service IG concerned of decisions in regards to applications from whistleblower reprisal complainants for the correction of military records.[75] BCMR officials told us that they are supposed to provide this notification on behalf of the service secretary but have not been consistently carrying out this responsibility. DODIG officials also told us that they are not aware of receiving any BCMR reports regarding case outcomes. However, DODIG also did not follow up with the services regarding this information because it had chosen not to track this information. DODIG therefore has had no visibility into or oversight capacity for this portion of the military whistleblower reprisal program. During the course of our review, however, DODIG officials acknowledged that they should be collecting and monitoring information on corrective action provided to whistleblowers and stated that they would begin doing so as part of their ongoing reforms to the whistleblower reprisal process.

DOD has a separate process for taking and tracking corrective action against those who have reprised against whistleblowers—also called command action. DOD Directive 7050.06 directs the secretaries of the military departments and the heads of the other DOD components to take corrective action based on the IG reports of investigations of military whistleblower reprisal allegations, and to notify DODIG of the action taken within 10 working days.[76] Further, DODIG requires that the service IGs report back to DODIG on command action taken against the subject—the individual alleged to have reprised against a whistleblower—according to officials from these organizations. DODIG records command action taken in its database and has reported in its semiannual reports to Congress examples of command action taken in response to substantiated military whistleblower reprisal claims.

While DOD Directive 7050.06 ultimately places responsibility for taking corrective action on the secretaries of the military departments based on the DODIG findings, it is up to a subject's military commanding officer to determine whether command action against the subject is appropriate, and if so, what form it should take. Military commanders are responsible for good order and discipline in their commands, and they have a number of judicial and administrative options at their disposal. DODIG officials told us that if a commander takes action against a subject in a military whistleblower reprisal case, it is largely, if not exclusively, an administrative action. Administrative actions are the least severe of the categories of command action available to the commander and can range from verbal counseling to written reprimands and demotion. Although DODIG has an important role in collecting information on and monitoring command action taken against subjects in response to substantiated whistleblower reprisal cases, DODIG has not been maintaining in its database reliable information on command action needed to fulfill this role. Specifically, DODIG data on command action indicates that almost half of all substantiated cases (40 percent) that were closed from October 1, 2005 through March 31, 2011, were awaiting reports from the services regarding the command action taken. According to most of the service IGs, they are diligent in providing command action information to DODIG on a timely basis. Data provided by the services showed that there were no cases pending follow-up action but we determined that the service data were not reliable enough for our purposes. However, DODIG officials also acknowledged that their information on command action was incomplete and that they were taking steps to both supplement data on existing closed cases and collect and maintain reliable data for command action taken in response to future substantiated cases. Until DODIG has reliable data on corrective action, DOD and Congress will be hindered in their ability to provide oversight of the corrective action portion of the military whistleblower reprisal program.

CONCLUSION

Whistleblowers play an important role in safeguarding the federal government against waste, fraud, and abuse, and Congress has enacted legislation to provide military whistleblowers with protections against reprisal. The requirements of the Military Whistleblower Protection Act provide complainants with a means to redress wrongs committed against them as a result of their whistleblowing; establish processes for holding subjects accountable; and provide the Secretary of Defense and decision makers with visibility over the military whistleblower reprisal investigative process and its outcomes. Recognizing problems with the process, and in response to its own internal review and a Department of Justice report it requested, the DODIG has expressed a renewed commitment to meeting the statutory timeliness and reporting requirements and ensuring quality investigations. Further, it has taken some steps to achieve these goals and to improve oversight of its investigations into allegations of reprisal against whistleblowers. Additional actions are needed, however. For example, recording, collecting, and tracking accurate, relevant data on case processing times would aid DOD in its efforts to identify inefficiencies or challenges to meeting timeliness requirements and in reporting to internal and external stakeholders. Finalizing the development and implementation of performance metrics for whistleblower reprisal investigations, such as ensuring case files contain evidence sufficient to support conclusions, would provide DOD with a means of ensuring that DOD is meeting its own standards for completing quality investigations. In addition, oversight actions—such as updating and adhering to the guidance governing investigations—could help improve the quality and oversight of reprisal cases. Finally, the overall purpose of DOD's whistleblower reprisal program is to identify servicemembers who have been reprised against, make them whole, and ensure that there are appropriate consequences for those who reprised against the whistleblower. This could be furthered if the DODIG and the service BCMRs develop processes and procedures to facilitate consideration of all substantiated allegations by the appropriate service BCMR. Increasing the completeness and reliability of data on corrective action could also provide DOD and Congress with information they need for oversight. Without addressing these issues, military whistleblowers may not be getting the full protection and resolution they deserve and DOD may not be reaping the full benefits whistleblowers could provide the department.

RECOMMENDATIONS FOR EXECUTIVE ACTION

To assist DOD with improving processing times of these investigations, we recommend that the Secretary of Defense work in coordination with DODIG to:

- implement policies and procedures to ensure accurate and complete recording and consistent tracking of total case processing time and processing time for various phases of the investigation;
- track and analyze timeliness data to identify reforms that could aid in processing cases within the 180 days provided by law; and

- regularly report to Congress on the timeliness of military whistleblower reprisal investigations, including the number of cases exceeding the 180 days provided by law. DODIG could do so in its semiannual reports.

To assist DOD in improving oversight over the whistleblower reprisal investigative process, we recommend that the Secretary of Defense work in coordination with DODIG to:

- develop and implement performance metrics to ensure the quality and effectiveness of the investigative process, such as ensuring that the case files contain evidence sufficient to support the conclusions;
- update whistleblower reprisal investigative guidance and ensure that it is consistently followed, including clarifying reporting requirements, responsibilities, and terminology; and
- consistently monitor the status of whistleblower reprisal investigations.

DODIG should work in close consultation with the service IGs when implementing these recommendations.

To better ensure that whistleblowers obtain the relief they are due, we recommend that the Secretary of Defense work in coordination with DODIG to identify best practices and develop the necessary processes and procedures to ensure that all whistleblower reprisal allegations substantiated by DODIG are considered under the whistleblower statute by the appropriate service BCMR. For example, DODIG could provide more detailed recommendations regarding corrective action for the complainant. DODIG should work in close consultation with the service IGs and the BCMRs when implementing this recommendation.

To ensure that the BCMRs are treating military whistleblower reprisal cases appropriately, given the unique procedural privileges provided by the Military Whistleblower Protection Act, we recommend that the Secretary of Defense direct the secretaries of the military departments to take action to ensure that military whistleblower cases are correctly identified and processed by the BCMRs. Such actions could include modifying the form used to apply to the BCMR; additional training so that BCMR staff can better identify cases; or developing methods for identifying cases for which the BCMRs have received DODIG substantiated case notifications.

To assist DOD in improving oversight of all corrective action taken in response to substantiated military whistleblower reprisal claims, including command action, we recommend that the Secretary of Defense work in coordination with DODIG to:

- establish standardized corrective action reporting requirements;
- consistently track and regularly reconcile data regarding corrective action; and
- regularly report to Congress on the frequency and type of corrective action taken in response to substantiated reprisal claims. DODIG could do so, for example, in its semiannual reports to Congress.

DODIG should work in concert with the service IGs and BCMRs when implementing these recommendations.

AGENCY COMMENTS AND OUR EVALUATION

In commenting on a draft of this report, DOD concurred with each of our recommendations. DOD also provided technical comments, which we considered and incorporated where appropriate.

In concurring with our recommendations that DODIG implement policies and procedures to ensure accurate and complete tracking of total case processing times and processing time for various phases of the investigation, track and analyze timeliness data, and regularly report to Congress on the timeliness of military whistleblower reprisal investigations, DOD stated that DODIG recognized the necessity of policies and procedures to ensure accurate and complete tracking of processing time for all phases of investigations and was taking multiple steps to address the GAO recommendations. These steps include modifying internal processes and updating policy manuals, redesigning the case management database, relying on data analysis to evaluate reforms and identifying further reforms, and reporting timeliness data to Congress. We believe that these steps, when fully implemented, could provide the department and the Congress with enhanced visibility over the status of military whistleblower reprisal investigations.

In concurring with our recommendations that DODIG develop and implement performance metrics, update and consistently follow guidance, and consistently monitor the status of military whistleblower reprisal cases, DOD stated that DODIG is taking steps to address each one of these areas, including revising its manual for administrative investigations to include clearly defined performance metrics, the required contents of investigative case files, as well as defining reporting requirements, responsibilities, and relevant terminology. It has also established a new oversight team which reviews and approves the determinations reached by the service IGs. DODIG is also in the process of establishing procedures that will directly monitor the progress of investigations and track command actions taken. We believe that the steps that DOD noted in its response could improve DOD's means of ensuring that DOD is meeting its own standards for completing quality investigations.

In concurring with our recommendation that DODIG, in close consultation with the service IGs and the BCMRs, identify best practices and develop the necessary process and procedures to ensure that all substantiated military whistleblower reprisal cases are considered by the appropriate BCMR, DOD stated that the mentioned organizations will begin meeting together within the next six weeks to identify best practices and develop an effective way forward. We acknowledge the department's stated commitment to these steps and encourage it to work toward the broad range of recommended steps, including that DODIG provide more detailed recommendations regarding corrective action for complainants.

In concurring with our recommendation that the service BCMRs take action to ensure that military whistleblower reprisal cases are correctly identified and processed by the BCMRs, DOD stated that the BCMRs will consider how to best ensure that whistleblowers with substantiated reprisal complaints are provided with all the information they need to determine if an application to a BCMR is appropriate. Although providing information to whistleblowers is a positive step, this alone will not address our finding that the service BCMRs are not consistently identifying applicants who have substantiated reprisal cases as such and are therefore not providing all reprisal victims with the procedural privileges to which they are entitled. Our recommendation included examples of possible actions the BCMRs could take to ensure that they are correctly identifying cases, including modifying the application form, additional training for BCMR staff, or developing methods for using the DODIG notification to BCMRs of substantiated cases as a way to flag military whistleblower reprisal cases, much like the Army BCMR does. We believe that improving the BCMRs' ability to properly identify substantiated military whistleblower reprisal cases could help to ensure that such cases are properly considered under the military whistleblower statute by the appropriate service BCMR.

In concurring with our recommendations that DODIG establish standardized corrective action reporting requirements, track and reconcile such data, and regularly report such information to Congress, DOD indicated that DODIG is redesigning its case management database to better enable it to record and report on such information. The overall purpose of DOD's whistleblower reprisal program is to identify servicemembers who have been reprised against, make them whole, and ensure that there are appropriate consequences for those who reprised against the whistleblower. We believe that the department's stated commitment to collecting and maintaining reliable data on corrective action—both for the remedies provided to complainants and command actions taken against subjects—and also regularly reporting such information to Congress could enhance oversight of the outcomes of the military whistleblower reprisal program.

Zina Merritt, Director
Defense Capabilities and Management

APPENDIX I: SCOPE AND METHODOLOGY

During our review of the Department of Defense's (DOD) military whistleblower reprisal program, we reviewed relevant documentation, gathered and assessed data, and met with representatives from numerous agencies, including the DOD Inspector General (DODIG), and Inspector General (IG) officials from the services (Army, Navy, Air Force, and Marine Corps).Table 9 lists all of the organizations we met with during our review. To determine DOD's process for investigating military whistleblower reprisals cases, we reviewed documents outlining investigative processes of DODIG and service IGs, including DODIG's investigative guide, and agency briefings and memoranda, and we spoke with officials from those organizations.[1]

Two primary sources of data used in several of our objectives were military whistleblower reprisal data from DODIG's database and from a random selection of DODIG closed military whistleblower reprisal case files. DODIG provided us with information for all military whistleblower reprisal cases opened and closed between fiscal year 2006 and the first half of fiscal year 2011 from the two databases they used to record these data.[2]

We combined the information from the two databases into one complete dataset, eliminating duplicate cases as per directions provided by DODIG.

Table 9. Organizations Met with During Review

Organization	Interviews conducted
DODIG	The Inspector General of the Department of Defense, Administrative Investigations, Office of Communications and Congressional Liaison, Whistleblower Reprisal Investigations Directorate,a Office of General Counsel, Office of Whistleblowing and Transparency
Army	Department of the Army Inspector General, Army National Guard Bureau Inspector General, U.S. Army Forces Command Inspector General, Army Board for Correction of Military Records
Air Force	Secretary of the Air Force Inspector General, Air Combat Command Inspector General, Air Force Reserve Command Inspector General, Global Strike Command Inspector General, Pacific Air Forces Inspector General, US Air Forces Europe Inspector General, 11 Wing Inspector General, Air Force Board for Correction of Military Records
Navy	Naval Inspector General; Commander, Navy Installations Command Inspector General; U.S. Fleet Forces Command Inspector General; Commander, Navy Reserve Forces Command Inspector General; Board for Correction of Naval Records
Marine Corps	Marine Corps Inspector General, Marine Corps Training and EducationCommand Inspector General, Marine Corps Third Marine Aircraft WingInspector General
Office of the Secretary of Defense	Office of the Under Secretary of Defense for Personnel and Readiness – Enterprise Services

Source: GAO.

[a] DODIG formed the Whistleblower Reprisal Investigations directorate during the course of our review when it merged the Military Reprisal Investigations and Civilian Reprisal Investigations directorates. We had previously met with the Military Reprisal Investigations directorate.

We also consulted with DODIG officials to ensure that we were properly identifying the various data elements.

In addition, we based our case file selection on the consolidated dataset of DODIG military whistleblower reprisal data. Specifically, a GAO statistician determined that a random sample of 97 cases from a list of the 871 military whistleblower reprisal cases DODIG closed between January 1, 2009 and March 31, 2011, would be appropriate. Our sample size of 97 cases was chosen to be generalizable, with a margin of error of 10 percentage points at the 95 percent confidence level for percentage estimates. We chose this time period because it represented DOD's most recent efforts and because DODIG had these files on site.3 Based on our review of whistleblower reprisal policies and procedures, we created a data collection instrument to identify the key characteristics of whistleblower reprisal cases, check the data reliability of the database information, and assess the completeness of files. We also developed a standard approach to reviewing files to ensure we reviewed all cases consistently. We refined this data collection instrument and our approach by first reviewing 12 case files that were not part of the 97 identified. Our methodology for reviewing the random sample required two analysts to review each case file, enter the information for each field in the data collection instrument, and transfer their information for each case to a central spreadsheet. We compared the two scores for each case, and highlighted the elements for which there was disagreement. Reviewers discussed the areas of disagreement and resolved any differences by identifying the necessary evidence in the case files. During the course of the case file review, our original sample size was reduced from 97 to 91 because 3 of the cases were found to be ongoing investigations, 2 cases were not military whistleblower reprisal cases, and DODIG could not locate 1 of the case files. However, this reduced sample is still generalizable, with an 11 percent margin of error at the 95 percent confidence level. Case file review results based on probability samples are subject to sampling error. The sample we drew for our case file review is only one of a large number of samples we might have drawn. Because different samples could have provided different estimates, we express our confidence in the precision of our particular sample results as a 95 percent confidence interval. This is the interval that would contain the actual population values for 95 percent of the samples we could have drawn. As a result, we are 95 percent confident that each of the confidence intervals in this report will include the true values in the study population. The margin of error associated with the confidence intervals of our case file review proportion estimates is no more than plus or minus 11 percentage points at the 95 percent level of confidence. The margin of error for any mean values based on our case file review will vary depending on the variability of the data and so is reported along with the mean.

In order to determine the extent to which DOD is meeting timeliness requirements for investigating military whistleblower reprisals, we reviewed relevant documents including The Military Whistleblower Protection Act, and its implementing directive on military whistleblower protections, DOD Directive 7050.06, *Military Whistleblower Protection* (Jul. 23, 2007). To identify possible challenges DOD faces in meeting these requirements, we reviewed key documents, including internal agency memos and briefings; the July 2009 Department of Justice Inspector General report; *A Review of the Department of Defense Office of Inspector General's Process for Handling Military Whistleblower Reprisal Allegations*; and DODIG's May 2011 *Review of the Office of Deputy Inspector General for Administrative Investigations, Directorate for Military Reprisal Investigations*. We also reviewed the 2010 DODIG report to Congress on progress made regarding recommendations from the Department of Justice review, and DODIG's October 2011 action plan in order to identify the steps DODIG has taken to address timeliness challenges. In order to determine if DOD was meeting statutory timeliness and reporting requirements, we conducted analysis of 91 randomly selected case files for cases closed between January 1, 2009 and March 31, 2011, (see above) and recorded the opening and closing dates indicated in the documentation for each case. We further reviewed those case files for evidence regarding timeliness reporting requirements. In order to determine the reliability of timeliness information in DODIG's database, we compared the opening and closing dates we determined by reviewing the case files to the opening and closing dates recorded for those cases in DODIG's database. We conducted checks to see whether DODIG database timeliness fields were filled out to determine if DODIG had reliable information on the time it takes to complete various investigative phases. In addition, we spoke with officials from DODIG and officials from the service IGs and the Office of the Under Secretary of Defense for Personnel and Readiness – Enterprise Services regarding timeliness issues, including compliance with timeliness reporting requirements.

In order to assess DODIG's actions to address overall process internal controls, we interviewed and discussed with DODIG officials their efforts to improve oversight of the whistleblower reprisal program. We also examined DODIG documents, including an internal review of the whistleblower reprisal program as well as their action plan to address oversight weaknesses. To assess DOD's oversight mechanisms used to safeguard the whistleblower reprisal investigative process, we reviewed key DOD guidance as well as relevant statutes and federal internal control guidance to include: the Military Whistleblower Protection Act codified at 10 U.S.C. § 1034, as amended, and DOD Directive 7050.06, *Military Whistleblower Protection* (Jul. 23, 2007); DOD Inspector General Office of the Deputy Inspector General for Investigations - Investigations Manual; GAO's *Standards for Internal Control in the Federal Government*; and the Council of the Inspectors General on Integrity and Efficiency, *Quality Standards for Investigations*, and discussed with DODIG officials their current practices. To assess DOD's adherence to its investigative process, we reviewed and discussed the DOD guidance mentioned above as well as the 1996 Inspector General Departmental Guidance (IGDG). In order to assess the completeness of DODIG's military whistleblower reprisal case files, we reviewed 91 randomly selected case files for cases closed between January 1, 2009 and March 31, 2011, (see above). To assess case file completeness, we reviewed DODIG's process, governing statute, directives, and other guidance and consulted with DODIG officials and identified 18 elements that we believe should be in case files. These 18 elements are necessary to either support the conclusions reached in the case, indicate compliance with the law or directive, or manage the case to include internal communication not specifically outlined by law or directive. The 18 elements we included for our case file review are the following:

1. Table of Contents Sheet
2. Database Coversheet
3. Investigation Oversight Worksheet
4. Correspondence between DODIG and the Service regarding the final outcome of the case
5. Correspondence between DOD and the complainant acknowledging receipt of the complaint
6. Correspondence between DOD and the complainant informing them of the outcome of the case
7. Investigation Analysis
8. Sequence of Key Events
9. Notification to DODIG from the Service IG that received the complaint
10. Interview Transcripts
11. Legal Review
12. Correspondence between DODIG and the Secretary of Defense regarding the final outcome of full investigations

13. Record of Corrective Action Taken
14. Army Oversight Worksheet
15. Correspondence between DODIG and the Secretary of Defense regarding investigations taking longer than 180 days
16. Correspondence between DODIG and the complainant regarding investigations taking longer than 180 days
17. Correspondence between DODIG and Congress acknowledging receipt of inquiry
18. Correspondence between DODIG and Congress informing them of the final outcome of the case

Some of these elements included specific documents. For example, the Army oversight worksheet (item 14 above) was a specific document. Other elements could be reflected in multiple documents. For example, the sequence of key events (item 8 above) could be in a larger report, be in a summary, or be its own document. Once we established the list, we further consulted with the director of DODIG's directorate responsible for conducting military whistleblower reprisal investigations to ensure that the elements selected were appropriate indicators of file completeness. The 18 elements were included in the data collection instrument and we used the methodology described above to gather information on these elements from the file. The completeness of each case file was determined individually since not all 18 elements were necessary in every case. For example, some of the 18 elements would only need to be present in a file if an investigation was conducted by a service, went beyond 180 days, or was a full investigation. We adjusted the required number of elements based on the specific circumstances of each case and calculated completeness based on that adjusted baseline. We categorized the case files as either complete (files with at least 85 percent of the case-specific elements present), partially complete (files with between 70 and 84 percent of the case-specific elements present), or incomplete (files with less than 70 percent of the case-specific elements present). To assess DODIG's monitoring of whistleblower reprisal investigations, we interviewed officials from DODIG as well as the IGs in each of the services.

In order to determine the roles and responsibilities of DODIG and the military services in providing corrective action, including the processes and procedures used by the Boards for Correction of Military Records (BCMRs) to provide relief to servicemembers who were reprised against, we reviewed applicable laws and regulations, including the Military Whistleblower Protection Act and DOD Directive 7050.06, and spoke with officials from

DODIG, the service IGs, the three service BCMRs, and the Office of the Under Secretary of Defense for Personnel and Readiness – Enterprise Services. In order to determine the extent to which servicemembers with substantiated cases apply for and receive relief from the service BCMRs, we compared a list of military whistleblower reprisal claims substantiated by DODIG between fiscal year 2006 and the first half of fiscal year 2011 to information in the databases of the service BCMRs. We created the list of substantiated military whistleblower reprisal claims from the database data provided by DODIG for cases closed between fiscal year 2006 and the first half of fiscal year 2011 and created a data collection instrument. We then went to each of the three service BCMRs with a list of substantiated cases specific to each BCMR's service. BCMR officials reviewed their database and provided resultant information for each individual case, which we then recorded in the data collection instrument. We also used the data collection instrument to identify the extent to which the service BCMRs were identifying military whistleblower reprisal cases as such in their case tracking system, the processing times for such cases, and the actions taken by the BCMRs to provide remedy to the complainant. In order to determine the reliability of the data, we spoke with BCMR officials to determine how the data in their database are processed. We also reviewed the data and performed logic checks. We found that the data were sufficiently reliable for our purposes. In order to identify the extent to which DODIG was tracking the relief provided to military whistleblowers, we spoke with officials from DODIG and the service IGs. In order to determine the extent to which the services took command action against those who have reprised against military whistleblowers, we reviewed DODIG data for cases closed between fiscal year 2006 and the first half of fiscal year 2011. We also obtained information from the service IGs regarding command action for all cases closed between January 1, 2009 and March 31, 2011. We chose this time frame based on the data retention practices of the service IGs. We determined the reliability of the DODIG and service IG data on relief by comparing them and through discussions with the officials and determined that the data were not reliable enough for our purposes.

In order to describe the military reprisal caseload for the period we reviewed, we obtained a copy of data from DODIG's database using the method described above. We assessed the reliability of the data, and then coded and derived statistical output.[4] We determined some to be reliable for our purposes, including the number of closed complaints, cases closed before full investigation, and not substantiated or substantiated cases. Other data were found to be not reliable enough for our purposes because they were either inaccurate or incomplete. To obtain additional information about DODIG's caseload, we conducted a case file review of military reprisal cases using the method described above.

We developed a data collection instrument and used it to record information on case characteristics located in the case files, including information about the complainant, the type of protected communication, unfavorable personnel action alleged to have occurred, and the reason for closing the case. As noted above, two analysts reviewed each case file and resolved any differences by identifying the necessary evidence in the case files.

We conducted this performance audit from April 2011 through February 2012 in accordance with generally accepted government auditing standards. Those standards require that we plan and perform the audit to obtain sufficient, appropriate evidence to provide a reasonable basis for our findings and conclusions based on our audit objectives. We believe that the evidence obtained provides a reasonable basis for our findings and conclusions based on our audit objectives.

Appendix II: General Information on Case Characteristics for Military Whistleblower Reprisal Investigations

This appendix provides information on the characteristics of military whistleblower reprisal cases based largely on both our review of files of cases closed between January 1, 2009 and March 31, 2011, as well as data from DODIG's database for cases closed between fiscal year 2006 and the first half of fiscal year 2011.

Complainant Characteristics for Closed Cases

Generally, neither the complainants' status as officer or enlisted nor their service matched their overall proportions in the military population. For example, complaints filed by officers made up approximately 31 percent of cases closed between fiscal year 2006 and the first half of fiscal year 2011, while officers constitute approximately 16 percent of the total military population.[1]

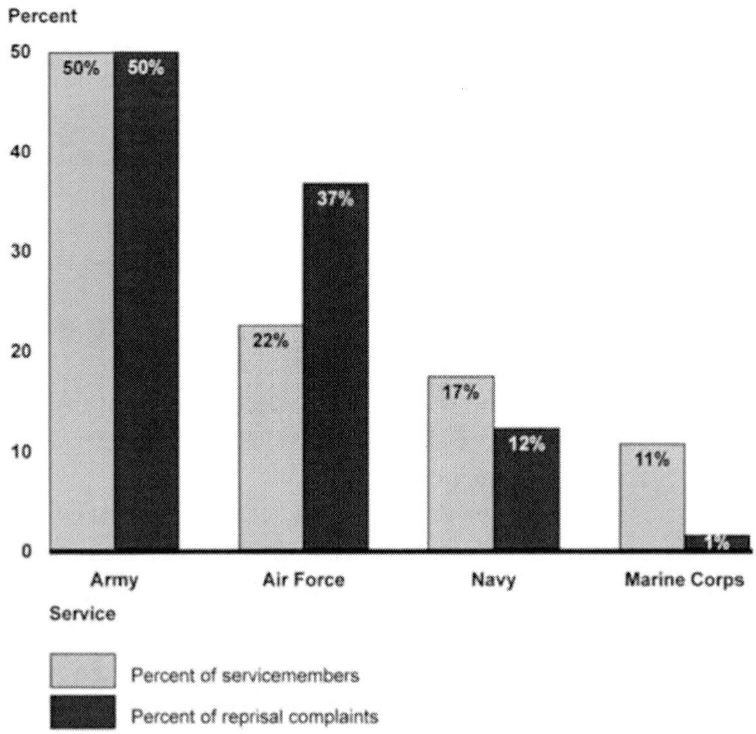

Source: GAO analysis of DODIG and DOD manpower data.

Notes:

Data to determine the percent of reprisal complaints by complainant service are based on GAO analysis of DODIG data on military whistleblower reprisal cases closed between fiscal year 2006 and the first half of fiscal year 2011. We did not include 1.6 percent of cases that were missing complainant service information or were coded as "Other" in DODIG's database.

The data to determine percentage of the total servicemember population for each service come from estimated fiscal year 2011 levels contained in DOD's "Defense Manpower Requirements Report – Fiscal Year 2011" (December 2010).

Figure 4. Relative Service Size vs. Percentage of Whistleblower Complaints by Service for Cases Closed between Fiscal Year 2006 and the First Half of Fiscal Year 2011.

Further, servicemembers from the Air Force filed approximately 37 percent of the complaints for cases closed between fiscal year 2006 and the first half of fiscal year 2011,[2] but made up only 22 percent of the military population. Servicemembers from the Navy and Marine Corps had the fewest closed complaints during this time period— 12 percent and 1 percent, respectively, while making up 17 percent and 11 percent of the military population.

The total number of closed reprisal complaints from servicemembers from the Army during this time period was higher than the other services but it was proportionate to the size of the Army. So although approximately 50 percent of military whistleblower reprisal complaints came from the Army during this time period, servicemembers from the Army also made up approximately 50 percent of the total military population. See figure 4 for a comparison of the servicemember population proportion by service compared to the proportion of reprisal cases closed.

Protected Communication Characteristics

According to DOD Directive 7050.06, a servicemember who makes or prepares to make a protected communication is a whistleblower. Our review of case files revealed that the primary reasons for making a protected communication are to report allegations of a violation of law or regulation (66 percent) or abuse of authority (44 percent).[3] DOD officials told us that regulations cover virtually every aspect of military life, including how to conduct personnel ratings, so complainants often cite violations of regulations in their complaints.

Officials from DODIG and the service IGs also told us that the vast majority of protected communications are not about allegations of significant fraud, waste, or abuse, such as reports of unnecessarily high costs of equipment or overpayment of contracts, but rather about relatively minor issues that only impact the individual complainant, such as supervisors not following regulations regarding a performance review. Our case file review revealed that this perception is not entirely accurate. We found that approximately one-third of complaints (36 percent) were concerned solely with personal issues; one-third of complaints (33 percent) concerned fraud, waste, or abuse issues; and one-third of complaints (31 percent) were a mix of the two.

The protected communications regarding allegations of fraud, waste, and abuse in the case files we reviewed tended to be about costs associated with misuse of government property, such as personal use of a government vehicle, or abuse of authority by commanders.

Unfavorable Personnel Action Characteristics

A whistleblower reprisal complaint must also include an allegation that an action was taken in reprisal against a servicemember. DOD Directive 7050.06 defines reprisal as taking or threatening to take an unfavorable personnel action, or withholding or threatening to withhold a favorable personnel action, for making or preparing to make a protected communication. [4] Based on our file review of cases closed between January 1, 2009 and March 31, 2011, the most common forms of reprisal alleged by complainants were that they received an unfavorable assignment or reassignment (50 percent), a poor performance evaluation (46 percent), or some sort of disciplinary action (42 percent).[5]

Reasons for Closing Cases

DODIG evaluates cases and generally closes them based on the answers to the four questions, referred to as the Acid Test (see fig. 2). Our review of randomly selected case files revealed that the most common reasons for closing a case were that DODIG determined that the complainant's actions not related to the protected communication justified the unfavorable personnel action (question 4 - 65 percent of closed cases), or that there was no unfavorable personnel action (question 2 - 41 percent of closed cases).[6] Based on our case file review, DODIG closed most complaints before conducting a full investigation and writing the resulting report of investigation (66 percent). DODIG data on cases closed between fiscal year 2006 and the first half of fiscal year 2011 show DOD closed a mean of 286 (71 percent) cases per year before conducting a full investigation, which is within the margin of error for our case file review.

Case Closure Rates

DODIG closed a mean of 405 military whistleblower reprisal cases a year between fiscal year 2006 and the first half of fiscal year 2011, ranging between a low of 325 closed cases and a high of 448 cases according to data provided by DODIG (see fig. 5).[7] We were not able to report on the military whistleblower reprisal cases received because we found that DODIG's data were not reliable for our purposes. As noted earlier, during our case file review, we observed that the case opening dates in DODIG's database did not match the opening dates documented in the case files. Without data on when cases were opened, we were unable to compare case opening and closure rates and determine if more cases were being opened or closed in any given year. Although we found the DODIG data to be reliable enough for our purposes in reporting total cases closed in a year, these figures do not match the data reported by DODIG in its semiannual reports to Congress. Those figures include more than military whistleblower reprisal cases, but adjusting for these additional cases does not fully make up the discrepancy between the figures in the semiannual reports and the data provided to us by DODIG. DODIG officials were not certain of the exact cause for the discrepancy and said that they did not have auditable data for their semiannual report figures for the time period we examined.

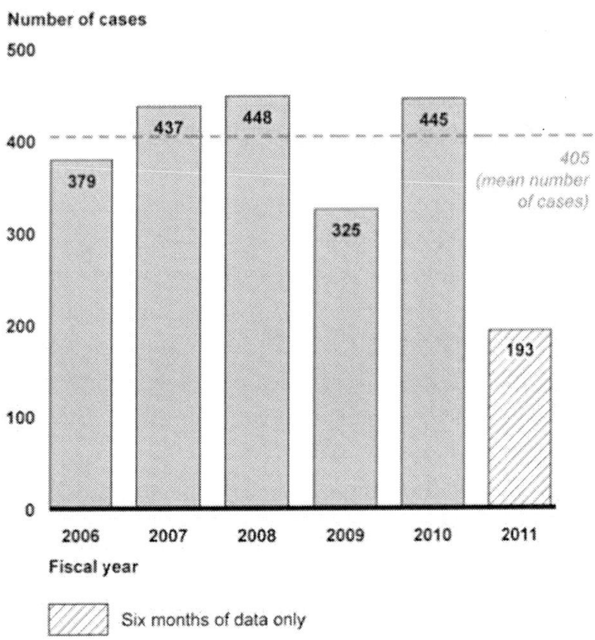

Source: GAO analysis of DODIG data between FY2006 and the first half of FY 2011.

Note: Fiscal year 2011 numbers reflect cases closed between October 1, 2010 and March 31, 2011.

Figure 5. Number of Closed Cases between Fiscal Year 2006 and the First Half of Fiscal Year 2011.

Full Investigation and Substantiation Rates

Our analysis of DODIG data on military whistleblower reprisal cases closed between fiscal year 2006 through the first half of fiscal year 2011 shows that DOD fully investigated a mean of 119 cases a year (29 percent of all cases), with 25 of those full investigations substantiated (6 percent of all cases), and 94 of those full investigations not substantiated (23 percent of all cases). DODIG determined that a mean of 286 cases a year (71 percent of all cases) did not warrant full investigation over the time period we reviewed. The number of full investigations ranged from a high of 156 in fiscal years 2006 and 2007 to a low of 69 in fiscal year 2009 and the number of substantiated cases ranged from a high of 40 in fiscal year 2006 to a low of 12 in fiscal year 2009 for cases closed during this time period.[8] Further, the number of full investigations and substantiated cases closed during this time period tended to be higher in the earlier fiscal years than the later fiscal years, with fiscal year 2009 being the lowest for both. Figure 6 shows the total cases closed by investigative phase for each fiscal year.

Further, the mean number of military whistleblower reprisal cases closed per year over this time period along with the number of cases fully investigated and substantiated varied by investigating organization according to data provided by DODIG. For example, the Army closed the highest number of cases per year (158 cases per year) and the Marine Corps closed the fewest cases per year (4 cases per year) over this time period.[9] The Air Force fully investigated the most cases per year (46 cases per year) and the Marine Corps fully investigated the fewest cases per year (2 cases per year) between fiscal year 2006 and the first half of fiscal year 2011. The Air Force and the Army substantiated the most cases per year (10 cases per year each) during this time period. The Marine Corps and DODIG substantiated the fewest cases per year (1 case per year each) over this time period. See figure 7 for the mean yearly number of closed cases by investigative phase and investigating organization for fiscal year 2006 through the first half of fiscal year 2011.

The percentage of total cases that are fully investigated and substantiated has generally declined between fiscal year 2006 and the first half of fiscal year 2011, reaching its lowest point in both cases in fiscal year 2009. Figure 8 shows the variation in the percentage of closed cases fully investigated by processing organization.10 DODIG's full investigation rate was lowest during this time period and it, along with the Air Force, had a generally steady full investigation rate whereas the Army and Navy full investigation rate generally declined over this time period.

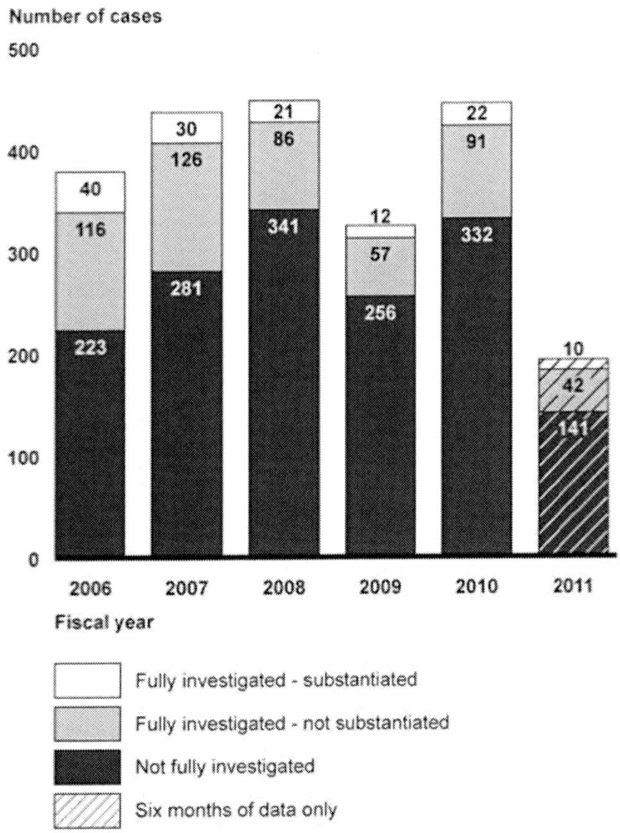

Source: GAO analysis of DODIG data between FY2006 and the first half of FY 2011.

Note: Data include two Army cases closed in fiscal year 2006 that were inappropriately coded in DODIG's database as substantiated military whistleblower reprisal cases.

Figure 6. Comparison of Substantiated, Not Substantiated, and Cases Not Fully Investigated for Military Whistleblower Reprisal Cases Closed between Fiscal Year 2006 and the First Half of Fiscal Year 2011.

Figure 9 also shows the variation by processing organization in the percentage of closed cases substantiated over this time period. In general, the substantiation rate declined, with DODIG having the lowest substantiation rate. However, there was some variation in the rate for each processing organization. Excluding the Marine Corps (see footnote 10), the Navy was the organization with the most variation, with substantiation rates ranging from 2 percent to 16 percent. DODIG was the organization with the least variation, with substantiation rates ranging from 0 percent to 3 percent.

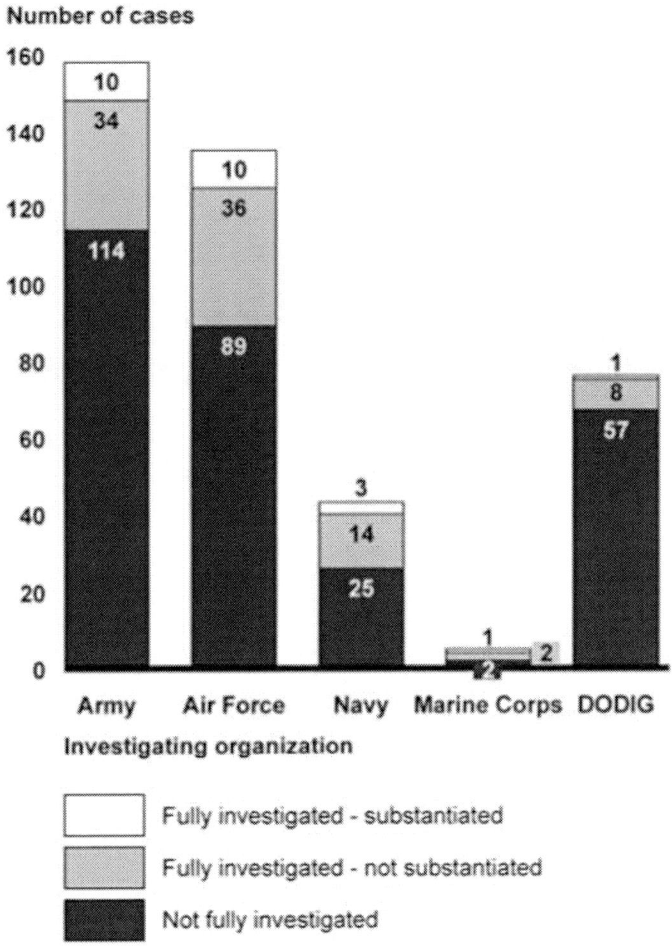

Source: GAO analysis of DODIG data between FY 2006 and the first half of FY 2011.

Notes:

Mean total number of cases for the Navy and Marine Corps do not match table 2 due to rounding.

Data presented here do not include seven cases closed over this time period where DODIG data for investigating organization is missing or listed as "Joint" or "Other."

Data include two Army cases closed in fiscal year 2006 that were inappropriately coded in DODIG's database as substantiated military whistleblower reprisal cases.

Figure 7. Mean Yearly Number of Closed Cases by Phase of Investigation and Investigating Organization between Fiscal Year 2006 and the First Half of Fiscal Year 2011.

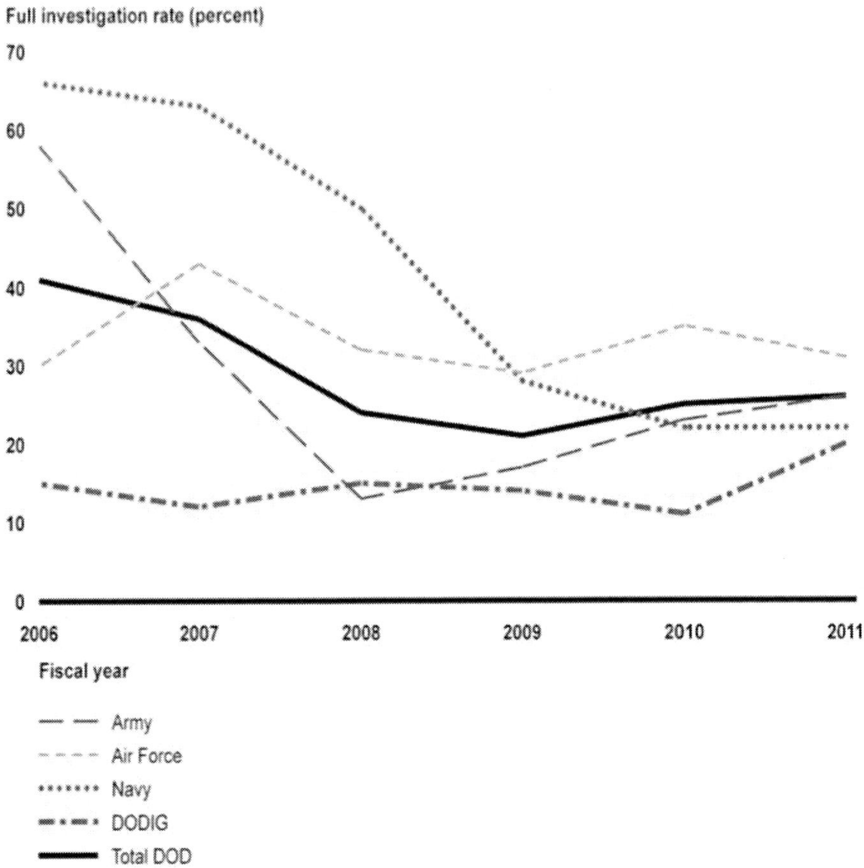

Source: GAO analysis of DODIG data between FY 2006 and the first half of FY 2011.

Notes:

Fiscal year 2011 numbers reflect cases closed between October 1, 2010 and March 31, 2011.

Marine Corps data were not shown due to the low number of cases closed and high variation in rates. Marine Corps data were included in the total.

Data presented here do not include seven cases closed over this time period where DODIG data for investigating organization are missing or listed as "Joint" or "Other."

Data include two Army cases closed in fiscal year 2006 that were inappropriately coded in DODIG's database as substantiated military whistleblower reprisal cases.

Figure 8. Percentage of Full Investigations out of Total Closed Investigations by Investigating Organization.

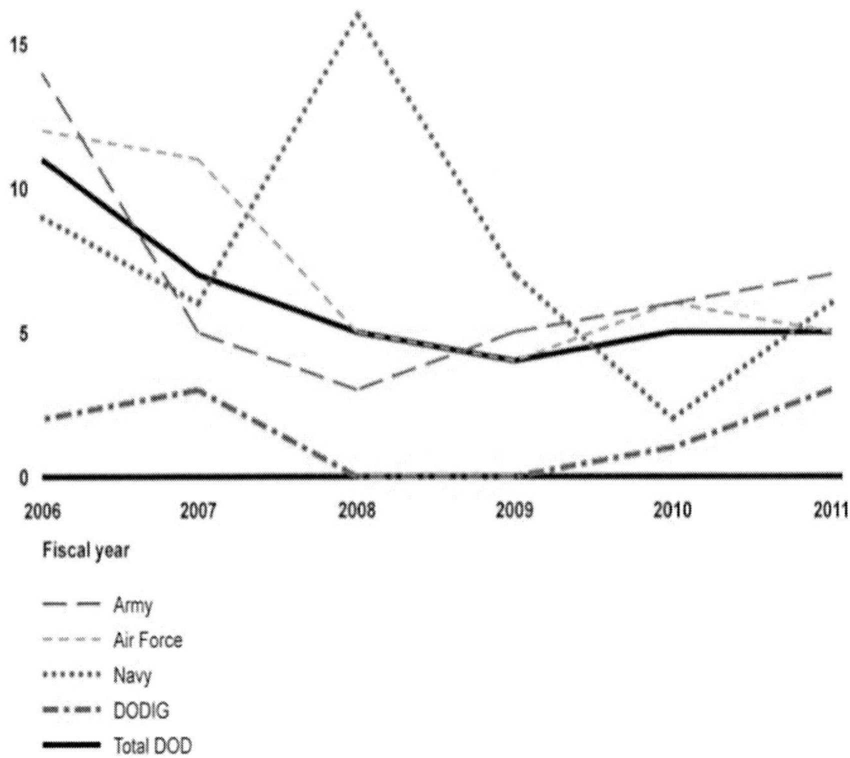

Source: GAO analysis of DODIG data between FY 2006 and the first half of FY 2011.

Notes:

Fiscal year 2011 numbers reflect cases closed between October 1, 2010 and March 31, 2011.

Marine Corps data were not shown due to the low number of cases closed and high variation in rates. Marine Corps data were included in the total.

Data presented here do not include seven cases closed over this time period where DODIG data for investigating organization are missing or listed as "Joint" or "Other."

Data include two Army cases closed in fiscal year 2006 that were inappropriately coded in DODIG's database as substantiated military whistleblower reprisal cases.

Figure 9. Percentage of Substantiated Investigations Out of Total Closed Investigations by Investigating Organization.

Appendix III: Comparison of Whistleblower Reprisal Cases That Were and Were Not Identified as Reprisal by Service BCMRs

	Number of cases (percent)	Mean days to close case	Cases over 180 days (percent)	Remedy provided (percent)
All cases				
Air Force	9	256	4	9
Army	6	167	2	3
Navy (all)	10	118	3	8
Navy	9	93	2	8
Marine Corps	1	338	1	0
Total	**25**	**179**	**9 (36%)**	**20 (80%)**
Cases identified as reprisal				
Air Force	4	230	2	4
Army	5	166	2	3
Navy (all)	6	40	0	5
Navy	6	40	0	5
Marine Corps	0	—	—	—
Total	**15 (60%)**	**133**	**4 (27%)**	**12 (80%)**
Cases not identified as reprisal				
Air Force	5	277	2	5
Army	1	168	0	0
Navy (all)	4	235	3	3
Navy	3	200	2	3
Marine Corps	1	253	1	0
Total	**10 (40%)**	**249**	**5 (50%)**	**8 (80%)**

Source: GAO analysis of DOD information.

Notes:

Based on DODIG data for cases that included military whistleblower reprisal allegations substantiated by DODIG between October 1, 2005 and March 31, 2011, and BCMR data regarding the cases submitted to them, including case outcomes.

Data do not include cases in which, according to DODIG data, the military whistleblower reprisal allegations are not substantiated but an improper referral for mental health evaluation (IMHE) is substantiated.

The Navy BCMR reviews cases for the Department of the Navy and therefore handles cases from both Navy personnel and Marine Corps personnel.

Two Navy BCMR cases—one from the Marine Corps and one from the Navy—were included and considered as not having received remedy although the Navy BCMR data are unclear whether or not it provided remedy. The Marine Corps case was not identified by the Navy BCMR as being a military whistleblower reprisal case. The Navy case was identified as a military whistleblower reprisal case.

Remedy provided indicates that the complainant received at least partial remedy. It does not indicate that the complainant received the exact remedy they were seeking.

End Notes

[1] National Defense Authorization Act, Fiscal Year 1989, Pub. L. No. 100-456, §846 (1988), codified at 10 U.S.C. § 1034, as amended.

[2] Specifically, 10 U.S.C. § 1034 prohibits individuals from restricting a member of the armed forces (hereafter referred to as servicemember) from making a lawful communication to a Member of Congress or an Inspector General (IG). It further prohibits individuals from taking or threatening to take an unfavorable personnel action, or withholding or threatening to withhold a favorable personnel action, as a reprisal against a servicemember for making or preparing to make a lawful communication to a Member of Congress or an IG or from communicating to a Member of Congress, IG, a member of a Department of Defense audit, inspection, investigation, or law enforcement organization; any person or organization in the chain of command; or any other person or organization designated pursuant to regulations or other established administrative procedures for such communications regarding what the servicemember reasonably believes to be evidence of any of the following: a violation of law or regulation, including a law or regulation prohibiting sexual harassment or unlawful discrimination, gross mismanagement, a gross waste of funds, an abuse of authority, or a substantial and specific danger to public health or safety.

[3] Department of Defense Directive 7050.06, Military Whistleblower Protection (Jul. 23, 2007) defines the military department IGs as including the IG of the Army, the Naval IG, the IG of the Air Force, and the Deputy Naval IG for Marine Corps Matters (Marine Corps IG). In this report, we refer to these organizations collectively as the service IGs.

[4] The Department of Justice IG review examined: (1) the statute and DOD regulations relating to military whistleblowers; (2) the allocation of responsibility for conducting investigations of military whistleblower reprisal allegations among the DODIG and the service IGs; (3) the management, staffing, and processes of the DODIG directorate responsible for military whistleblower reprisal investigations; (4) the quality of DODIG's investigative product and its oversight of the service IGs' processing and investigation of reprisal complaints; and (5) the effectiveness of DODIG in satisfying its legal obligations and ensuring that reprisal allegations are thoroughly and fairly investigated.

[5] U.S. Department of Justice, Office of the Inspector General, A Review of the Department of Defense Office of Inspector General's Process for Handling Military Whistleblower Reprisal Allegations (July 2009).

[6] We selected a random sample of 97 cases from a list provided by DODIG of a total of 871 military whistleblower reprisal cases closed between January 1, 2009 and March 31, 2011. However, we had to exclude 6 cases from our analyses because they were not accurately characterized in DODIG's database. Specifically, 3 cases were ongoing investigations, 2 cases were not military whistleblower reprisal cases, and DODIG could not locate 1 case file.

[7] Data from DODIG were for all military whistleblower reprisal cases closed between fiscal year 2006 and the first half of fiscal year 2011 (October 1, 2005 through March 31, 2011).

[8] Data from the service IGs were for all military whistleblower reprisal cases closed between January 1, 2009 and March 31, 2011.

[9] The Navy's BCMR also reviews cases brought to it by members of the Marine Corps.

[10] Data from the service BCMRs were for all military whistleblower reprisal cases closed by DODIG between fiscal year 2006 and the first half of fiscal year 2011.

[11] Department of Defense Directive 7050.06, Military Whistleblower Protection (Jul. 23, 2007).

[12] Allegations of an improper referral of a servicemember for a mental health evaluation are subject to different laws and regulations, although referrals for mental health evaluations are included in the definition of personnel action, for the purposes of alleging a reprisal under Department of Defense Directive 7050.06.

[13] A nonappropriated fund instrumentality (NAFI) employee is a civilian employee who is paid from nonappropriated funds of the Army and Air Force Exchange Service, Navy exchanges Service Command, Marine Corps exchanges, or any other instrumentality of the United States under the jurisdiction of the armed forces which is conducted for the comfort, pleasure, contentment, or physical or mental improvement of members of the armed forces.

[14] DODIG had a separate directorate to investigate whistleblower reprisal allegations filed by civilians, but this directorate was merged in October 2011with the directorate responsible for whistleblower reprisal investigations for servicemembers (military whistleblower reprisal), contractors, and nonappropriated fund employees, as well as improper referrals of servicemembers for mental health evaluations.

[15] DOD Directive 7050.06 defines DOD components as including the following organizational entities: Office of the Secretary of Defense, the Military Departments, the Chairman of the Joint Chiefs of Staff, the Combatant Commands, DODIG, the Defense Agencies, the DOD Field Activities, and all other organizational entities within DOD.

[16] Section 5 of appendix 3 of Title 5 of the United States Code requires each inspector general to prepare semiannual reports summarizing the activities of the office during the immediately preceding 6-month period ending March 31 and September 30, no later than April 30 and October 31 of each year. The law specifies that the report is to include, among other things, a description of significant problems, abuses, and deficiencies relating to the administration of programs and operations of that establishment.

[17] DOD Directive 7050.06 Section E2.9 defines protected communication and lists the appropriate officials as a Member of Congress, an IG, or a member of a DOD audit, inspection, investigation, or law enforcement organization, or any person or organization in the chain of command; or any other person designated pursuant to regulations or other established administrative procedures to receive such communications.

[18] DOD Directive 7050.06 Section E2.8 defines a personnel action as any action taken on a servicemember that affects, or has the potential to affect, that military member's current position or career. Such actions include a promotion; a disciplinary or other corrective action; a transfer or reassignment; a performance evaluation; a decision on pay, benefits, awards, or training; referral for mental health evaluations under DOD Directive 6490.1; and any other significant change in duties or responsibilities inconsistent with the military member's grade.

[19] Under 10 U.S.C. §1034 (c)(4) IGs at DOD are not required to investigate allegations that are made more than 60 days after the date the servicemember becomes aware of the unfavorable personnel action that is alleged to have occurred as a result of reprisal. According to Section E3.1.1 of DOD Directive 7050.06, while no investigation is required in those cases, an authorized IG receiving such a complaint may, nevertheless, consider the complaint based on compelling reasons for the delay in submission or the strength of the evidence submitted.

[20] 10 U.S.C. §1034 (i) also includes the Department of Homeland Security (DHS) IG as a qualifying IG, in the case of a member of the Coast Guard when the Coast Guard is not operating as a service in the Navy. According to DODIG officials, they do not have any record of a Coast Guard military whistleblower reprisal allegation and are not aware of any such complaints brought by a member of the Coast Guard to the DHS IG.

[21] DODIG officials told us that cases of special interest could include high-profile cases, including those with congressional interest and cases that involve a complainant from one service and a subject from another.

[22] DOD Inspector General Departmental Guidance 7050.6, Guide to Investigating Reprisal and Improper Referrals for Mental Health Evaluations, (Feb. 6, 1996). In this report we refer to this document as the DODIG investigative guide.

[23] U.S. Department of Defense Inspector General, "Review of the Office of Deputy Inspector General for Administrative Investigations, Directorate for Military Reprisal Investigations," May 2011.

[24] Under 10 U.S.C. §1034 (e)(3), the IG investigating a military whistleblower reprisal investigation must complete an investigation report within 180 days. If the investigating IG determines it is not possible to complete the report within 180 days of the date the allegation under investigation was made, the IG must notify the complainant and the Secretary of Defense that this deadline cannot be met and of the reasons why, as well as a time when the report will be completed.

[25] DOD Directive 7050.06, Military Whistleblower Protection (July 23, 2007).

[26] The Defense Hotline is a DODIG program responsible for taking in all types of complaints for DOD in addition to whistleblower reprisal complaints. Its activities are governed by Department of Defense Instruction 7050.01, Defense Hotline Program (Dec. 17, 2007). The Defense Hotline receives and investigates complaints or information concerning allegations of violations of law, rules or regulations, mismanagement, gross waste of funds, abuse of authority, and a substantial and specific threat to the public health and safety involving the Department of Defense.

[27] The new approach is a beta-test where DODIG allows its investigators to speak with subjects at the onset of an inquiry or initial analysis to determine if the case warrants full investigation. The previous process did not allow investigators to speak with subjects unless the case definitely went to full investigation.

[28] The 2009 Department of Justice IG report recommended that DODIG consider whether it should take responsibility for conducting the initial review for the incoming complaints from all of the services, not just those from the Army. In its October 2011 action plan, DODIG stated it would assess how well the service IGs are performing intake of reprisal complaints in late fiscal year 2012 and that DODIG would evaluate the Department of Justice IG recommendation that DODIG consider conducting initial reviews of all service reprisal complaints after it has implemented some of its other reforms.

[29] The Army IG also expressed concerns that process reforms made by DODIG since early 2011 had reversed gains the Army IG was beginning to see in the processing of military whistleblower reprisal complaints.

[30] Although case processing time for the full sample is generalizable, it is not generalizable for any subset. Additionally, the case processing time data reported for the two investigative phase subsets are based on 89 of the 91 cases we analyzed. For the investigative phase subsets, we excluded 2 additional cases because we could not identify the investigative phase in which they were closed based on the evidence in the case file.

[31] For the subset of inquiries closed before full investigation, the median days to close a case was 249, with a range from 14 to 2,215 days. For full investigations, the median days to close a case was 349, with a range from 51 to 1,181 days.

[32] 10 U.S.C. §1034 (e)(3) requires the IG investigating the allegation of reprisal to submit to the Secretary of Defense and the complainant a notice if they determine it is not possible to submit an investigative report within 180 days after receiving the allegation. The notice to

the Secretary of Defense and the complainant is to contain a determination that the report may not be submitted on time and the reasons for the delay, as well as the time when the report will be submitted. DOD Directive 7050.06 assigns responsibility for providing these reports to DODIG. The directive also directs the service IGs to submit reports of investigation to DODIG within 180 days and if unable to do so, directs them to provide notice to the DODIG in addition to the complainant and the office designated to receive notice on behalf of the Secretary of Defense. The directive requires DOD component IGs other than the service IGs to provide DODIG with a report of investigation within 180 days from the date DODIG requested an investigation, but does not require them to provide notice if the 180 day time frame is exceeded.

[33] DOD Directive 7050.06 requires the investigating organization to submit notice to the complainant as well as to the Deputy Under Secretary of Defense for Program Integration within the Office of the Secretary of Defense. Responsibility for receiving notices was shifted to the Office of the Under Secretary of Defense for Personnel and Readiness—Enterprise Services in December 2011 (see table 1 on roles and responsibilities).

[34] DODIG officials could not recall when they stopped sending the notifications to the Secretary of Defense for investigations that were not closed within 180 days of the date the allegation was made. Officials from the office currently responsible for receiving these notifications (Office of the Under Secretary of Defense for Personnel and Readiness— Enterprise Services) had no record of receiving such notifications. Further, our case file review of 91 cases closed between January 1, 2009 and March 31, 2011, included 64 cases that were not closed within 180 days. We did not find evidence in any of these 64 case files that the Secretary of Defense had been notified. However, we did find evidence in 2 of the 64 cases of notifications sent to complainants.

[35] Council of the Inspectors General on Integrity and Efficiency, Quality Standards for Investigations (Nov. 15, 2011). The Council of the Inspectors General on Integrity and Efficiency gets its authority from Section 11 of the Inspector General Act of 1978 (5 U.S.C. app. 3.), as amended. The mission of the Council of the Inspectors General on Integrity and Efficiency shall be to address integrity, economy, and effectiveness issues that transcend individual government agencies and increase the professionalism and effectiveness of personnel by developing policies, standards, and approaches to aid in the establishment of a well-trained and highly skilled workforce in the Offices of Inspectors General.

[36] GAO, Personnel Security Clearances: Progress Has Been Made to Improve Timeliness but Continued Oversight Is Needed to Sustain Momentum, GAO-11-65 (Washington, D.C.: Nov. 19, 2010).

[37] From our analysis of a random sample of cases closed between January 1, 2009 through March 31, 2011, we estimate that DODIG accurately recorded the case received dates 30 percent of the time and accurately recorded the case closed dates 93 percent of the time.

[38] We considered cases to have accurate dates if the dates in the database and supporting documentation in the actual case file matched for both the received and closed dates.

[39] GAO, DOD Personnel Clearances: Comprehensive Timeliness Reporting, Complete Clearance Documentation, and Quality Measures Are Needed to Further Improve the Clearance Process, GAO-09-400 (Washington, D.C.: May 19, 2009).

[40] GAO, Standards for Internal Control in the Federal Government, GAO/AIMD-00-21.3.1 (Washington, D.C.: Nov. 1, 1999).

[41] According to section 3 of appendix 3 of Title 5 of the United States Code, each Inspector General shall report to and be under the general supervision of the head of the establishment involved or, to the extent such authority is delegated, the officer next in rank below such

head, but shall not report to, or be subject to supervision by, any other officer of such establishment.

[42] DOD Directive 7050.06 (July 23, 2007).

[43] Department of Defense Directive 5106.01, Inspector General of the Department of Defense (Apr. 13, 2006), establishes that the Inspector General of the Department of Defense shall report to and be under the general supervision of the Secretary of Defense and the Deputy Secretary of Defense, but shall not report to, or be subject to supervision by, any other officer of the Department of Defense. The directive also states that neither the Secretary of Defense nor the Deputy Secretary of Defense shall prevent or prohibit the Inspector General of the Department of Defense from initiating, carrying out, or completing any audit, evaluation, inspection, or investigation, unless otherwise specified in law.

[44] See 5 U.S.C. App. 3, §5 and Department of Defense Directive 5106.01, par. 5.17 (Apr. 13, 2006).

[45] U.S. Department of Justice, A Review of the Department of Defense Office of Inspector General's Process for Handling Military Whistleblower Reprisal Allegations (July 2009).

[46] U.S. Department of Defense Inspector General, Review of Office of Deputy Inspector General for Administrative Investigations, Directorate for Military Reprisal Investigations (May 2011).

[47] GAO, Standards for Internal Control in the Federal Government, GAO/AIMD-00-21.3.1 (Washington, D.C.: Nov. 1, 1999).

[48] GAO, Internal Control Management and Evaluation Tool, GAO-01-1008G (Washington, D.C.: Aug. 2001).

[49] GAO, DOD Personnel Clearances: Comprehensive Timeliness Reporting, Complete Clearance Documentation, and Quality Measures Are Needed to Further Improve the Clearance Process, GAO-09-400 (Washington, D.C.: May 19, 2009).

[50] GAO, Whistleblower Protection: Sustained Management Attention Needed to Address Long-standing Program Weaknesses, GAO-10-722 (Washington, D.C.: Aug.17, 2010).

[51] DOD Inspector General Office of the Deputy Inspector General for Investigations, Investigations Manual Reprisal and Senior Official Cases (Mar. 2006).

[52] Council of the Inspectors General on Integrity and Efficiency, Quality Standards for Investigations (Nov. 15, 2011).

[53] DOD Inspector General Departmental Guidance 7050.6, Guide to Investigating Reprisal and Improper Referrals for Mental Health Evaluations (Feb. 6, 1996).

[54] GAO-01-1008G.

[55] As noted previously, the Military Whistleblower Protection Act and DOD Directive 7050.06 both allow alternative notification to the Secretary of Defense and the complainant if the 180 days provided by law are going to be exceeded.

[56] Council of the Inspectors General on Integrity and Efficiency, Quality Standards for Investigations (Nov. 15, 2011).

[57] DOD Inspector General Office of the Deputy Inspector General for Investigations, Investigations Manual Reprisal and Senior Official Cases (March 2006).

[58] Some of these elements included specific documents. For example, the Army oversight worksheet was a specific document. Other elements could be reflected in multiple documents. For example, the sequence of key events could be in a larger report, be in a summary, or be its own document. For further details on our methodology, see app. I.

[59] DOD Inspector General Departmental Guidance 7050.6, Guide to Investigating Reprisal and Improper Referrals for Mental Health Evaluations (Feb. 6, 1996).

[60] See: GAO/AIMD-00-21.3.1.

[61] Department of Defense Directive 7050.06 assigns those responsibilities to the DODIG and includes, within the definition of "DOD Components": the Office of the Secretary of Defense, the Military Departments, the Chairman of the Joint Chiefs of Staff, the Combatant Commands, the Office of the Inspector General of the Department of Defense, the Defense Agencies, the DOD Field Activities, and all other organizational entities within the Department of Defense.

[62] DOD Directive 7050.06 sections 5.3.3 and 5.4.2 (Jul. 23, 2007).

[63] 10 U.S.C. §1034.

[64] Officials from each of the BCMRs told us that they review thousands of cases a year and that reprisal cases in any year run in the single digits.

[65] In this report, when we refer to the first half of fiscal year 2011, we mean between October 1, 2010 and March 31, 2011.

[66] Our review of a random sample of case files closed between January 1, 2009 and March 31, 2011, found one case where restriction was substantiated and one where the threat of an unfavorable personnel action was substantiated. Neither complainant brought their case to a BCMR for review and remedy.

[67] Data obtained from the Air Force BCMR showed that the Air Force Evaluation Report Appeals Board provided partial remedy to one applicant who had a military whistleblower reprisal case substantiated by DODIG between fiscal year 2006 and the first half of 2011. However, that applicant also obtained additional remedy from the Air Force BCMR.

[68] 10 U.S.C. § 1034, as amended.

[69] The BCMRs are the highest level of administrative review in the services.

[70] According to BCMR officials, servicemembers with cases that are not whistleblower reprisal have to challenge BCMR decisions in federal court.

[71] GAO/AIMD-00-21.3.1.

[72] The service BCMRs have adopted different interpretations of what cases qualify as a reprisal case. DOD Directive 7050.06 requires secretaries of the military departments to ensure that BCMRs shall consider applications for the correction of military records at the request of servicemembers or former servicemembers who allege that they have been reprised against due to their whistleblower activity. The Air Force BCMR considers anyone with a reasonable whistleblower reprisal claim to be a whistleblower with the corresponding procedural privileges. The Army and Navy BCMRs consider only applicants with cases substantiated by DODIG as whistleblowers. Other cases that may include whistleblower allegations that are not substantiated are reviewed under each BCMR's regular authority. Army officials added that, should the Army BCMR ultimately determine that an applicant's reprisal case has merit even if it was not substantiated by DODIG, the Army BCMR has the ability to invoke its authority under the Military Whistleblower Reprisal Act.

[73] In GAO/NSIAD-95-23, Whistleblower Protection: Continuing Impediments to Protection of Military Members (February 1995), we reported that at that time BCMRs were unable to identify any specific whistleblower cases because they were not uniquely coding them. As a result of a settlement in a 1977 court action, DOD and service directives required the BCMRs to establish a single index system for all BCMR cases except those involving characterizations of discharge. The system was to provide a means for applicants to identify or isolate cases that may be similar to theirs and indicate the grounds for which the BCMR or Secretary granted or denied relief. The Department of the Army was responsible for developing the initial format of the index system, establishing joint facilities for inspection, and copying opinions. We therefore recommended that the BCMRs establish the required code. According to Army BCMR officials, in 2002 the court approved DOD's request to

discontinue standardized BCMR indexing of cases because the new data systems used by the BCMRs fulfilled the underlying purpose for the court order.

[74] GAO/AIMD-00-21.3.1.

[75] DOD Directive 7050.06, Section 5.3.8 (July 23, 2007).

[76] DOD Directive 7050.06 Sections 5.3.3 and 5.4.2 (July 23, 2007).

End Notes for Appendix I

[1] DOD Inspector General Departmental Guidance 7050.6, Guide to Investigating Reprisal and Improper Referrals for Mental Health Evaluations, (Feb. 6, 1996).

[2] At the time DODIG provided us the data, it kept information on reprisal cases in two databases. DODIG used the CASES database to record information for all cases that it investigated and those cases that went to full investigation. DODIG used the separate Service IG Reprisal Case (SIRC) database to record information on military whistleblower reprisal cases reviewed by the service IGs. However, if those service cases went to full investigation, DODIG would close the case in SIRC and reopen the case in CASES. In October 2011, DODIG began phasing out the use of its SIRC database by recording information on all new cases in its CASES database. Although DODIG used two databases to record information, in this report we generally refer to the information from these databases as data from the DODIG database (singular).

[3] DODIG officials stated that their file retention policy is to keep files on site for the current year and the 2 previous calendar years before files are sent to an off-site archive.

[4] To assess the reliability of data elements, we performed database checks for missing fields and incorrect entries. We also verified that the investigative phases in which cases were closed (before full investigation, full investigation - not substantiated, and full investigation - substantiated) were recorded correctly through information we pulled during our case file review. We coded the data according to direction provided by agency officials at DODIG.

End Notes for Appendix II

[1] Percentage of closed complaints where the complainant was an officer is based on DODIG provided data for military whistleblower reprisal cases closed between fiscal year 2006 and the first half of fiscal year 2011. Note: We included the 10 percent of cases in the database that did not have data on the complainant's rank so the percentage of closed complaints from officers is at a minimum 31 percent, but could be higher. Percentage of officers in the total military population was obtained from Department of Defense, "Defense Manpower Requirements Report – Fiscal Year 2011" (December 2010).

[2] Figures for percentage of cases closed by complainant service exclude 1.6 percent of cases that were missing complainant service information or were coded as "Other" in DODIG's database.

[3] Percentages do not add up to 100 percent because complainants can allege multiple protected communications.

[4] A protected communication is any lawful communication to a Member of Congress or an IG or a communication made to certain appropriate officials that the individual reasonably

believes evidences violation of law or regulation, including a law or regulation prohibiting sexual harassment or unlawful discrimination, gross mismanagement, a gross waste of funds or other resources, an abuse of authority, or a substantial and specific danger to public health or safety.

[5] Percentages reported on reprisal types do not add up to 100 percent because complainants often allege multiple reprisal types.

[6] Percentages reported on reasons for closing cases do not add up to 100 percent because one complaint often includes multiple allegations and investigators often cite multiple reasons for closing a case.

[7] Our data for fiscal year 2011 go only through the first half of that year. Assuming the total number of cases for the second half were similar to the 194 cases closed in the first half, fiscal year 2011 totals would fall within the range noted.

[8] Our data for fiscal year 2011 go only through the first half of that year. Assuming the number of fully investigated and substantiated cases for the second half were similar to the 52 fully investigated and 10 substantiated cases closed in the first half, fiscal year 2011 totals would fall within the ranges noted.

[9] The numbers reported in this paragraph may not match those reported in fig. 7 due to rounding of each investigative phase number in fig. 7.

[10] For both figs. 8 and 9 we did not include the data for the Marine Corps because the low number of cases processed by the Marine Corps caused small variations in the number of cases fully investigated and substantiated to show up as large percentage variations. The Marine Corps data were included in the totals in both figures.

In: Whistleblower Protections
Editor: Daryl R. Arcelloni

ISBN: 978-1-62417-211-3

Chapter 4

TAX WHISTLEBLOWERS: INCOMPLETE DATA HINDERS IRS'S ABILITY TO MANAGE CLAIM PROCESSING TIME AND ENHANCE EXTERNAL COMMUNICATION*

The United States Government Accountability Office

ABBREVIATIONS

CI	Criminal Investigation
IRS	Internal Revenue Service
JCT	Joint Committee on Taxation
LB&I	Large Business and International Division
NOL	Net Operating Loss
SB/SE	Small Business / Self Employed Division
SME	subject matter expert
TE/GE	Tax Exempt and Government Entities Division
TIGTA	Treasury Inspector General for Tax Administration
W&I	Wage and Investment Division

---

* This is an edited, reformatted and augmented version of The United States Government Accountability Office publication, Report to Congressional Requesters GAO-11-683, dated August 2011.

Why GAO Did This Study

The Tax Relief and Health Care Act of 2006 expanded the Internal Revenue Service's (IRS) whistleblower program, increasing rewards for submitting information on others' tax underpayments to up to 30 percent of collected proceeds. The expanded program targets tax underpayments over $2 million and could reduce the gap between taxes owed and taxes paid. IRS's Whistleblower Office has received over 1,300 submissions qualifying for this new program since 2007.

GAO was asked to assess (1) how IRS manages the expanded program, (2) how IRS communicates with whistleblowers and the public, and (3) any lessons from IRS's or other government whistleblower programs that could improve IRS's expanded whistleblower program. GAO analyzed IRS documents and data and interviewed IRS officials, whistleblower attorneys, and federal and state whistleblower program officials.

What GAO Recommends

GAO recommends that IRS collect more information—including data on the time each step takes for all claims and reasons for claim rejection—in its claim tracking system, establish a process to follow up on claims that exceed review time targets, and include more information on these issues in its annual reports to Congress.

In written comments on a draft of this report, IRS generally agreed with our recommendations.

What GAO Found

Whistleblower claims can take years to go through the IRS review and award determination process. As of April 2011, about 66 percent of claims submitted in the first 2 years of the program, fiscal years 2007 and 2008, were still in process. According to IRS officials, claims can take years to process because IRS must take various steps to ensure the integrity of claim reviews and resulting taxpayer examinations. Further, taxpayers subject to examination can exercise rights that can add years to the process. IRS does not collect complete data on the time each step takes or the reasons claims are rejected.

Without such data, IRS may be unable to identify potential improvements to claim processing efficiency. Furthermore, not all the IRS divisions that review whistleblower claims have time targets for their subject matter expert reviews. Nor does the Whistleblower Office have a systematic process to check in with the divisions about the time taken for their initial reviews.

IRS Expanded Whistleblower Program Claim Review Process Steps

1. Whistleblower files claim
2. Whistleblower Office initial claim review
3. Subject matter expert review
4. Classification and examination
5. Appeals and collections
6. Period for taxpayer to exercise right to request refund
7. Whistleblower Office final review
8. Award payment

Source: GAO analysis of IRS documents and the Internal Revenue Manual.

IRS is limited in what information it can share with whistleblowers about the status of claims because of statutes protecting the privacy of tax information. For example, because IRS cannot disclose if it is examining a taxpayer, it cannot inform whistleblowers on the progress of their claims or the reasons their claims are rejected. One mechanism through which the Whistleblower Office can communicate program results is its mandated annual report to Congress. However, the most recently released report, for fiscal year 2010, did not contain information on case processing times or specific data on why IRS rejected claims. Collecting additional data and including it in the report could improve the transparency of the program and Congress's ability to oversee it.

Federal and state whistleblower programs have features with potential benefits that could improve IRS's expanded whistleblower program, including options that increase interaction or information shared with whistleblowers and options that attempt to improve the accountability for claim processing. While there are potential advantages to all identified options, it is difficult to determine if the advantages outweigh the disadvantages for many options. Furthermore, IRS would be limited by taxpayer data protections in implementing some of the options.

August 10, 2011

The Honorable Max Baucus
Chairman

The Honorable Orrin Hatch
Ranking Member
Committee on Finance United States Senate

The Honorable Charles E. Grassley
Ranking Member
Committee on the Judiciary
United States Senate

For decades the Internal Revenue Service (IRS) has had the authority to pay awards to whistleblowers who submit information about others' tax underpayments. The Tax Relief and Health Care Act of 2006[1] expanded this authority to make it more attractive for whistleblowers to provide information to IRS, which could help IRS reduce the tax gap—the difference between what is owed in taxes and what is paid voluntarily and on time. IRS's most recent estimate of this gross tax gap was $345 billion for 2001.[2] The act, which targets tax amounts in dispute of more than $2 million, requires IRS to pay whistleblowers up to 30 percent of the collected proceeds, including additional tax, interest, penalties, and other amounts it collects as a result of information whistleblowers provide. The act also directed IRS to establish a Whistleblower Office to administer the expanded whistleblower program. Since the Whistleblower Office was established in early 2007, IRS has received over 1,300 whistleblower submissions qualifying for the expanded program, alleging tax noncompliance by more than 9,500 taxpayers. As of May 12, 2011, IRS has paid a small number of awards under the expanded program. IRS has determined that information on awards paid is protected from disclosure in the same manner as taxpayer return information and disclosure of the number of awards paid would violate IRS's privacy protections.[3]

You asked us to review IRS's expanded whistleblower program to determine whether it is operating effectively and to what extent improvements could be made. In response, this report's objectives are to:

1) assess how IRS manages the expanded whistleblower program;
2) evaluate how IRS communicates with whistleblowers and the public; and (3) determine what lessons, if any, can be learned from IRS's and whistleblowers' past experiences with the Whistleblower Office and other governmental efforts that could improve IRS's expanded whistleblower program.

To assess how IRS manages the expanded whistleblower program, we analyzed the Internal Revenue Manual and other IRS documents and data, interviewed officials from IRS's Whistleblower Office and operating divisions which investigate whistleblower claims, and reviewed GAO's existing body of work on internal control standards. To evaluate how the Whistleblower Office communicates with whistleblowers and the public, we interviewed IRS officials and private attorneys who represent multiple tax whistleblowers. To determine what lessons can be learned from IRS's and others' experiences with whistleblower cases, we reviewed documents and interviewed officials from federal agencies and state tax agencies with whistleblower reward programs.

We also interviewed attorneys who represent tax whistleblowers to discuss their experiences with submitting whistleblower claims to IRS. Whistleblower attorneys have a clear financial interest in the outcome of whistleblower claims. However, interviewing them allowed us to obtain broad viewpoints of the IRS whistleblower program while keeping whistleblowers' identities confidential. For more information on our scope and methodology, see appendix I.

We conducted this performance audit from September 2010 to August 2011 in accordance with generally accepted government auditing standards. Those standards require that we plan and perform the audit to obtain sufficient, appropriate evidence to provide a reasonable basis for our findings and conclusions based on our audit objectives. We believe that the evidence obtained provides a reasonable basis for our findings and conclusions based on our audit objectives.

BACKGROUND

In 1867, Congress enacted legislation that allowed the government to pay awards to individuals who provided information that aided in detecting and punishing those guilty of violating tax laws.[4] Initially, Congress appropriated funds to pay these awards at the government's discretion.

Table 1. Current Features of IRS's Original and Expanded Whistleblower Programs

Feature	Original program	Expanded program
Date of whistleblower claim submission	All submissions made before December 20, 2006, and submissions that do not otherwise meet criteria for the expanded program	Submissions made December 20, 2006, or laterthat also meet the amounts in dispute criteria below
Threshold criteria for tax amount in dispute	Submissions made on or after December 20, 2006, where amount in dispute is $2 million or less in tax underpayments; no threshold for submissions made prior to December 20, 2006	Submissions where amount in dispute is over $2 million; if claim is against an individual, the individual must also have more than $200,000 in gross income for at least one tax year covered by the claim
Award payment	Discretionary award up to 15 percent of collected proceeds, capped at $10 million by IRS for claims submitted prior to December 20, 2006; for claims submitted after July 1, 2010, award determination will be based on the criteria that apply to the expanded program	Mandatory award, generally between 15 percent and 30 percent of collected proceeds with no award cap[a]
Basis of award calculation	Additions to tax, penalties, and other amounts collected as a result of administrative or judicial action resulting from the information provided	Additions to tax, penalties, interest, and other amounts collected as a result of any administrative or judicial action resulting from the information provided
Venue for appealing award determinations	None[b]	U.S. Tax Court[c]

Source: GAO analysis of Internal Revenue Code section 7623 and IRS documents.

[a] Award calculations begin at a base of 15 percent and are adjusted up or down due to certain positive or negative factors. For example, award calculations can be increased to up to 30 percent for whistleblowers who show extraordinary cooperation or assistance in providing information to IRS. Awards are reduced to a maximum of 10 percent if the information was gathered primarily from judicial or administrative hearings.

[b] Whistleblowers may appeal determinations under the original program to the Court of Federal Claims if IRS had entered into a contract, written or implied, with the whistleblower, and the contract comes into dispute.

[c] Section 7623(b)(4) of the Internal Revenue Code provides the Tax Court jurisdiction to hear appeals of award determinations, including the amount or denial of an award, under the expanded program. See Cooper v. Commissioner, 135 T.C. 70 (July 8, 2010).

In 1996, Congress expanded the scope of the program to also provide awards for detecting underpayments of tax and changed the source of awards to money IRS collects as a result of information whistleblowers provide.[5]

The Tax Relief and Health Care Act of 2006 created an expanded whistleblower award program to complement the existing whistleblower program.[6] Table 1 shows the distinctions between the two programs, which we refer to as the original and expanded programs. This report focuses on the expanded program.

The act also directed IRS to create the Whistleblower Office, which is responsible for managing and tracking whistleblower claims from the time IRS receives them to the time it closes them, either through a rejection letter or an award payment. The Secretary of the Treasury is required to submit an annual report to Congress on the activities and outcomes of both the original and expanded whistleblower programs. As of May 2011, the Whistleblower Office had 20 staff members.

IRS's review of whistleblower claims involves a series of steps and IRS can reject claims throughout the process. Although IRS's Whistleblower Office manages the whistleblower program, conducts initial reviews of claims, and makes award determinations, IRS's operating divisions are responsible for investigating claims and conducting examinations under the expanded program.[7] The Office of Chief Counsel is not involved in every whistleblower claim but reviews whistleblower claims for legal issues when the Whistleblower Office or operating divisions request such assistance. IRS's Criminal Investigation (CI) unit also investigates fraud identified by whistleblower claims.[8] A claim may transfer from CI to an operating division if CI is initially involved but declines to pursue the claim. Conversely, an operating division can involve CI if it determines during an examination that there is a criminal component to a claim. While the act establishing the expanded whistleblower program does not offer specific protections for whistleblowers, the Whistleblower Office has several policies and procedures to protect the identity of a whistleblower.

Whistleblowers may not submit claims anonymously, as submissions must be made under penalty of perjury and IRS needs to assess the credibility of whistleblowers and the information they provide. Likewise, certain individuals, such as some federal employees, are prohibited from receiving whistleblower awards and the Whistleblower Office must know the identity of the whistleblower to enforce this restriction. Table 2 is a simplified outline of the whistleblower claim process for the expanded program.

Table 2. Expanded Whistleblower Program Claim Process Steps and Potential Outcomes

Claim process step	Step description	Potential outcomes
Step 1 Whistleblower files claim	A whistleblower files Form 211, Application for Award for Original Information, with Whistleblower Office	
Step 2 Whistleblower Office initial claim review	The Whistleblower Office reviews Form 211 and assesses if the claim qualifies for the expanded whistleblower program	(1) The claim does not meet expanded criteria and is processed using the original program rules; (2) The claim does not qualify for the original or expanded program; whistleblower receives a Whistleblower Office rejection letter—case closed; or (3) The Whistleblower Office refers the claim to the appropriate operating division
Step 3 Operating division subject matter expert (SME) review	SMEs perform an initial assessment to determine whether the allegation is worthwhile to pursue and ensure that documents received are not privileged	(1) The SME rejects the claim as something IRS will not pursue; whistleblower receives a Whistleblower Office rejection letter—case closed; or (2) The SME forwards the claim to the operating division examination function
Step 4 Operating division classification and examination	The operating division determines how a claim fits into its overall examination workload, may perform an examination, and determines the change in tax assessment, if any; when completed, operating division sends award claim file to the Whistleblower Office	(1) An examination is not included in the workload for various reasons, such as other priority examinations or the issue was reviewed in a prior examination; the case is sent back to the Whistleblower Office; whistleblower receives a Whistleblower Office rejection letter—case closed; or (2) An examination concludes with no change in tax assessment;award claim file is sent back to the Whistleblower Office; whistleblower receives a Whistleblower Office rejection letter—case closed; or (3) An examination concludes with a revised assessment for the taxpayer

Table 2. (Continued).

Step 5 Appeals and collections	(1) The taxpayer may appeal the assessment within IRS or the courts; or (2) The taxpayer pays the tax and, if any, penalties and interest	(1) The taxpayer wins the appeal and has no change in tax liability; whistleblower receives a Whistleblower Office rejection letter—case closed; or (2) The taxpayer loses the appeal or does not appeal; IRS collects monies
Step 6 Taxpayer right to request refund	Taxpayers have the right to request a refund within 2 years from the date the tax was paid	The Whistleblower Office waits to make an award determination until the allowable time for the taxpayer to request a refund has expired, which is typically 2 years
Step 7 Whistleblower Office final review	The Whistleblower Office determines an award percentage and notifies the whistleblower of the intended award amount	(1) The determination shows the whistleblower's information did not contribute to any tax recovery; whistleblower receives a Whistleblower Office rejection letter—case closed; or (2) The whistleblower receives a notification letter indicating the intended award
Step 8 Award payment	The Whistleblower Office pays the whistleblower	Whistleblower is paid a taxable sum—case closed

Source: GAO analysis of IRS documents and Internal Revenue Manual.

Whistleblower awards are mandatory if IRS takes administrative or judicial action that results in collected proceeds based on the whistleblower's information. IRS is clarifying the definition of collected proceeds. Currently, the Internal Revenue Manual section on whistleblower awards defines collected proceeds as only new monies collected.[9] Recently, IRS issued proposed regulations that would clarify the definition of collected proceeds to include denials of refunds and reductions in overpayment credit balances when calculating a whistleblower's award.[10] If IRS pays an award to a whistleblower, its policy is to withhold 28 percent in tax from all whistleblower payments, as award payments are taxable income.[11] IRS withholds tax to reduce the risk of tax underpayment on what can potentially be large amounts of income.

At the federal level, there are several other agencies that offer awards for those who bring forth information that could lead to the government recouping money. The Department of Justice receives allegations of fraud against the government under the False Claims Act, although tax cases are specifically excluded. The False Claims Act includes a qui tam provision that allows whistleblowers to pursue claims on behalf of the government if the government elects not to proceed on the claims brought by the whistleblower. The Centers for Medicare and Medicaid Services offers awards to those who provide information on health care fraud. The Securities and Exchange Commission and the Commodity Futures Trading Commission are each implementing whistleblower programs and consulted IRS for advice.[12] Three states—New York, Florida, and Texas—also have tax whistleblower reward programs. New York's program has a tax qui tam provision that was enacted in August 2010. Oregon also has a tax whistleblower reward statute, but the program is inactive.

WHISTLEBLOWER CLAIMS CAN TAKE YEARS TO PROCESS BUT THE WHISTLEBLOWER OFFICE DOES NOT HAVE COMPLETE DATA ON CLAIM PROCESSING TIME

Whistleblower claims can take years to go through the IRS review and award determination process. For example, as of April 25, 2011:

- about 66 percent of claims submitted in the first 2 years of the program, fiscal years 2007 and 2008, were still in process;
- less than 7 percent of claims submitted in fiscal years 2007 and 2008 that were still in process were in the Whistleblower Office final review or Whistleblower Office award evaluation steps; and
- 447 claims submitted in fiscal year 2010 had been in the Whistleblower Office initial claim review step at least 200 days.

For each year since 2007, table 3 shows the number of claims at each step of the review process as tracked within E-TRAK, a claim management information system IRS developed and launched in January 2009. The table does not include claims receiving awards because of IRS's concerns about disclosing tax information.

According to Whistleblower Office and operating division officials, it can take IRS significant time to review and examine whistleblower claims for various reasons.

Table 3. Status of Whistleblower Claims by Identified Taxpayers by Year of Claim Receipt, Fiscal Years 2007 to 2011

	FY 2007	FY 2008	FY 2009	FY 2010	FY 2011[a]	Total
Total number of whistleblowers	50	362	430	389	156	1,387
Total claims (taxpayers identified by whistleblowers)	561	1,183	2,016	5,358	422	9,540
Number of claims rejected	24	574	537	140	11	1,286
Number of claims in process	537	609	1,479	5,218	411	8,254
• Whistleblower Office initial claim review	0	0	0	447	121	568
• Operating division SME review	2	73	117	933	157	1,282
• Criminal Investigation review	2	4	17	18	3	44
• Operating division examination	498	274	541	425	121	1,859
• Taxpayer appeals	7	3	6	2	0	18
• Whistleblower Office final review	12	52	98	45	2	209
• Whistleblower Office award evaluation	1	12	19	4	0	36
• Claim suspended[b]	15	191	681	3,344[c]	7	4,238

Source: GAO analysis of IRS data.

Notes: E-TRAK currently tracks claims by taxpayers identified. Some whistleblowers submit information on multiple taxpayers in one submission. For approximately 200 submissions made prior to July 2008, E-TRAK assigned multiple taxpayers to one claim. The data in the table, therefore, generally refer to the number of alleged noncompliant taxpayers and not the number of whistleblowers, except in the row labeled "total number of whistleblowers." All data are as of April 25, 2011, and do not include data on claims receiving awards.

[a] Fiscal year 2011 covers the period from October 1, 2010, through April 25, 2011.

[b] Suspended claims are those that are awaiting action outside of IRS's or the Whistleblower Office's control. Claims may be classified as suspended during the collections process or while the Whistleblower Office waits for the statute of limitations for taxpayers to request refunds to expire. Claims may also be suspended if a submission involved more than one taxpayer and IRS has yet to complete all related taxpayer examinations. E-TRAK does not actively track the reasons why claims are suspended.

[c] In fiscal year 2010, the Whistleblower Office received one whistleblower submission that identified more than 3,000 taxpayers. Most of these taxpayer claims were placed in suspended status while the operating divisions evaluate if they will pursue a claim for each identified taxpayer.

- Some whistleblower claims are highly complex and are submitted with large amounts of supporting documentation. Evaluating large amounts of data is time-consuming.
- Both the Whistleblower Office and the SMEs need to understand the relationship between a whistleblower and a target taxpayer in order to make determinations about the qualifications of the claim. For example, certain individuals are not eligible for awards under the expanded whistleblower program, including federal employees who learn of tax noncompliance in the course of their work activities or individuals who are current representatives, such as attorneys or accountants, of a targeted taxpayer.
- SMEs review information that whistleblowers provide to determine if it may be tainted, meaning it may be subject to attorney-client privilege or any other legal protections that would preclude IRS from using it in an examination. If SMEs determine that information may be tainted, the Office of Chief Counsel reviews the claim and determines which documents should and should not be forwarded to an examination team.
- SMEs can request debrief meetings with whistleblowers to clarify the tax noncompliance issues alleged or to determine the source of submitted information to ensure it is not privileged. According to operating division officials, arranging and holding these meetings can add time to the SME review process; for example, if IRS counsel is not immediately available or whistleblowers need to arrange to travel to an IRS office.
- SMEs have other work priorities that may delay their review of whistleblower claims. SMEs may have expertise in specific areas of tax compliance, such as employment tax or estate and gift tax. LB&I, SB/SE, and TE/GE have between 7 and 10 SMEs each; they do not work exclusively on whistleblower claims and support other examinations and IRS programs.[13]
- Within the examination step, operating divisions do not prioritize whistleblower claims; they are treated the same as all other examinations.14 According to IRS officials, each claim should rise on its own merits alongside other cases that have been selected for examination by other programs.

After the examination step, whistleblowers will likely still have to wait several years before IRS can determine if they are due an award due to factors outside the Whistleblower Office's control. Taxpayers can appeal IRS's assessment of tax, and if a taxpayer and IRS cannot reach agreement on the outcome of the case through the appeals process, the taxpayer may have the case reviewed by the U.S. Tax Court, U.S. Court of Federal Claims, or a U.S. district court.

Furthermore, the Whistleblower Office generally does not pay claims until after IRS collects all proceeds from taxpayers, the 2 years taxpayers are granted to request refunds of their payments has elapsed, and in some cases, IRS has completed all taxpayer examinations resulting from a single award claim form (Form 211).

Whistleblower Office officials said that the 2-year wait was important because taxpayers, regardless of whether they were the subject of a whistleblower investigation, have the right to request a refund, even on issues that whistleblowers identified.[15] Likewise, the officials said that waiting until all claims under one submission are complete can be to the benefit of whistleblowers if, for example, claims only meet the disputed tax amount criteria for the expanded program when considered in aggregate.[16] Other than for claims being appealed, IRS classifies these types of claims in E-TRAK as suspended.

Table 3 provides data on the number of claims that were in suspended status as of April 25, 2011.

We also identified other factors that could affect claim processing times. As discussed, Whistleblower Office analysts and SMEs review the relationship of a whistleblower to a targeted taxpayer when assessing the credibility of information whistleblowers provide. Although Form 211 asks whistleblowers to explain their relationship to target taxpayers, the question is part of a broader question asking whistleblowers to describe the documents they provided.

Operating division SMEs told us that sometimes the relationship information is not provided or is included within the attached documents, where it can take significant time to find and understand the relationship. Furthermore, Form 211 does not ask other questions that help IRS evaluate whistleblowers' submissions, such as if the whistleblowers have supplied the same information to other government agencies, submitted all information they have supporting a claim, or are federal employees. Operating division officials told us that having this relationship and other information more clearly identified at the beginning of the whistleblower claim review process could help them process claims more efficiently.

The Whistleblower Office Does Not Have Complete and Accurate Data on Claims Processing, Including Time in Each Step

Although table 3 highlights the length of time taken to review claims, the Whistleblower Office does not collect complete and accurate data in ETRAK about several aspects of claims processing that could be used to manage the whistleblower program. For example, the Whistleblower Office and operating divisions do not have complete data on the length of time claims spend at each step of the review process to inform the decision making for establishing appropriate review time targets. We requested aggregate data on the median time claims spend in each step by fiscal year of claim receipt and data on how often the Whistleblower Office and subject matter experts complete the initial reviews within a given number of days, but Whistleblower Office officials told us time data from E-TRAK would be incomplete for various reasons.

First, the Whistleblower Office does not update E-TRAK with data on time taken for each step for all claims. If one submission includes claims for multiple taxpayers, the Whistleblower Office updates time information for only one master claim within the submission and references all related claims to the master claim. E-TRAK records time data for related claims only if the time in a step for a related claim diverges from that of the master claim. Without significant data analysis, Whistleblower Office officials are not able to determine how often this divergence occurs.

Therefore time data cannot be reported on a per-claim or per-whistleblower-submission basis, but can be reported as a combination of the two.

Second, IRS did not consistently record time data for submissions before the introduction of E-TRAK in January 2009.[17] Time data on claims that completed each step before this date are incomplete; while time data may have been recorded for some submissions, it was not required for all submissions. Whistleblower Office officials stated that E-TRAK was designed to be a claim management tool to track claim progress rather than one designed to report and monitor overall program performance. According to one Whistleblower Office official, IRS does not use aggregate time information in the day-to-day operations of the program and, therefore, did not build these capabilities into E-TRAK when designing it. Because E-TRAK already has the data field available for tracking time information, the cost of tracking such information for all claims would be limited to the time needed for analysts to input the additional data field in the claim file.

Other aspects of E-TRAK limit the accuracy of Whistleblower Office data. For example, E-TRAK may show more time than is accurate for some claim review process steps because of E-TRAK's method for accounting for certain events. The Whistleblower Office can perform an initial review and assign a claim to a SME for review. If a SME later returns the claim to the Whistleblower Office to be reassigned to a different operating division, E-TRAK does not reset the day count on how long the claim has been with the Whistleblower Office. E-TRAK will show the day count for Whistleblower Office initial review as the time the claim was received until the time the claim was reassigned to the second operating division for review. Similarly, if a SME requests legal advice from Chief Counsel's Office, E-TRAK continues to count the time the claim is with Chief Counsel's Office as being with the SME.

Table 4. Rejected Claims by Taxpayers Identified by Step in Process Where Rejection Occurred, Fiscal Year 2007 to 2011

Step in process
Whistleblower Office initial review
SME review
Examination
Suspended
Whistleblower Office final review[a]
Not tracked[b]
Total

Source: GAO analysis of IRS data.

Notes: Fiscal year 2007 data begins with the program's inception date of December 20, 2006. Fiscal year 2011 data includes data through April 25, 2011.

[a] Generally, IRS does not reject claims in the examination step. When IRS completes an examination, examiners send an award claim file to the Whistleblower Office and the Whistleblower Office analysts determine how useful the whistleblower's information was to the examination outcome based on information the examiner provided. The Whistleblower Office rejects claims where an examination concluded with no change in assessment or where a whistleblower's information did not contribute to an examination.

[b] Claims rejected before January 2009 were not tracked by the step in the review process where rejection occurred and are listed in the table as "not tracked."

The Whistleblower Office only began tracking the point in the process at which whistleblower claims were rejected in January 2009, when E-TRAK was introduced. As table 2 showed, IRS can reject whistleblower claims at almost any point in the process. For example, claims may not fit the criteria for the award program, IRS may already have the information the whistleblower submitted, or an examination may result in no change in tax assessed, among other reasons. Table 4 shows the breakdown of when in the process IRS rejected claims. Of the claims where the rejection step was tracked, over half were rejected after examination in the Whistleblower Office final review. All claims that were rejected before January 2009 are labeled as not tracked in table 4.

Although the Whistleblower Office has begun to track the step in the claim review process at which claims are rejected, E-TRAK does not include data fields for tracking the reasons why claims are rejected, although the information is contained in the text fields of the claim files. Without reviewing all closed claims, Whistleblower Office management cannot know how frequently claims are rejected for each reason. Tracking this information could help the Whistleblower Office make some program management or resource allocation decisions and in reporting information. For example, whistleblower attorneys we interviewed were concerned that claims that take years to process risk being rejected because the statute of limitations for assessment may expire before IRS completes an examination.[18] Whistleblower Office officials could not provide E-TRAK data on the exact number of times claims are rejected because the statute has expired because E-TRAK does not track why claims are rejected, but they stated that it is not a frequent outcome.[19] Without data in E-TRAK on rejection reasons, the Whistleblower Office cannot know how frequently claims are rejected because the statute has expired. Whistleblower Office officials said that while this information would be helpful, collecting it is not yet a priority.

Furthermore, IRS could not provide data on specific reasons why claims were suspended because E-TRAK only tracks this information in the comments section of claim files, which do not require standardized language to allow for accurate searching, according to a Whistleblower Office official. Without this data in E-TRAK, Whistleblower Office officials did not know how many claims were in the 2-year period during which the taxpayer can request a refund. Having such information may aid the Whistleblower Office in planning for future work related to likely award payments. Adding a field to E-TRAK to capture both reasons why claims are in suspended status and why they were rejected would likely require limited resources to reprogram E-TRAK.[20] Additional limited resource needs would include the time needed for analysts to input the reason when updating the claim file.

Having more complete data available to Whistleblower Office management would be consistent with key internal control standards for maintaining relevant and reliable information to help agencies achieve their objectives.[21] Without complete and accurate data on claim processing time, the Whistleblower Office may not be able to identify certain aspects of the program, if any, that could be improved to increase claim processing efficiency. Moreover, according to IRS's overall strategic goals for 2009-2013, the agency should act quickly to initiate compliance contacts, complete audits, and collect taxes in order to reduce the administrative burden on IRS and reduce overall costs, such as penalties and interest, for the taxpayer. This lack of complete data limits the Whistleblower Office's ability to provide program information to Congress and the whistleblower community, which may erode confidence in the program.

The Whistleblower Office Does Not Have a Systematic Process to Manage the Timeliness of All the Processing Steps It Oversees

Whistleblower claims can take years to process due in part to steps (some required) outside the Whistleblower Office's control, such as examinations of taxpayers' returns, taxpayer appeals, and taxpayer rights to request a refund up to 2 years after making a payment. However, the Whistleblower Office can do more to manage the time taken for the parts of the process it does influence. The Whistleblower Office and some operating divisions have time targets for their initial claim reviews; however, other operating divisions do not have targets and the Whistleblower Office does not have a systematic process to check in on claims once they are with the operating divisions for review. To monitor the time taken for the Whistleblower Office initial claim review step, the Whistleblower Office established a target of 60 days to review a claim.

Claims in the Whistleblower Office initial review step more than 60 days are flagged in E-TRAK, which triggers an inquiry by Whistleblower Office analysts and management to determine and validate the reason for the delay. SB/SE and CI have targets for SME reviews, at which point claims that eclipse the target are flagged for follow-up. SB/SE's target, which was formally established in March 2011, is a series of 30-day targets for various activities of the SME review process, such as the process for reviewing information for taint concerns and optional debrief meetings with whistleblowers. SB/SE's overall target is 240 days and CI's target is 90 days to perform the initial SME review. Whistleblower Office officials could not provide complete data on how often claims meet these targets. LB&I and TE/GE do not have targets for how long initial reviews should take, although TE/GE policy directs SMEs to follow up on all claims at least once quarterly and LB&I SMEs report to their managers on claims over 200 days old.

The Whistleblower Office does not have a systematic process to check in with the operating divisions to review claims based on the length of time they have been in the SME review step, and the operating divisions do not have full access to E-TRAK to be able to generate reports on claims assigned to them. Without a systematic process to check in on all claims, the Whistleblower Office risks having claims not receiving the attention or resources they need to be completed, and operating division management may not have the information needed to make effective SME resource allocation decisions. Whistleblower Office officials told us they send a list of claims inventory to each operating division monthly, ordered by oldest claim first. They further stated that this report is only for informational purposes because the Whistleblower Office does not have the resources to check in with the operating divisions regularly on specific claims. Operating division officials told us they do not receive this report monthly but may receive it quarterly, or sometimes less frequently. Some SMEs have had access to E-TRAK to update information since September 2010, but they are limited in what information they can input or search, making it incumbent on the Whistleblower Office to provide to them certain data about assigned claims. The Whistleblower Office plans to allow SMEs greater access to E-TRAK in the future. For example, LB&I officials told us they are working with the Whistleblower Office to expand their E-TRAK access to allow them to directly run their own reports from E-TRAK, including reports that could show claims that have been in the SME review step the longest.

RESTRICTIONS ON DISCLOSING TAX INFORMATION LIMIT IRS COMMUNICATION ON SPECIFIC CLAIMS, BUT INCREASED COMMUNICATION ON OVERALL RESULTS COULD IMPROVE PROGRAM TRANSPARENCY

IRS is limited in what information it can share with whistleblowers and other stakeholders throughout the whistleblower claim process. Section 6103 of the Internal Revenue Code prohibits the unauthorized disclosure of tax information.[22] According to IRS, disclosing to a whistleblower that IRS is examining a taxpayer reveals tax information; therefore, IRS does not inform whistleblowers on the progress of their claim other than to confirm that the claim is either open or closed. Furthermore, IRS does not publicly report or comment on specific whistleblower awards, which it also considers to be tax information. IRS will report only on aggregate whistleblower award information once the Whistleblower Office has paid a number of awards sufficient to avoid improper disclosure.

Because section 6103 restricts IRS in the amount of information it can share with whistleblowers and whistleblower claims can take years to resolve, whistleblowers may not hear from the Whistleblower Office for years once claims are accepted. According to Whistleblower Office officials, even though IRS tells whistleblowers about the restrictions on providing status updates and the potential for claims to take years to complete, the Whistleblower Office fields numerous calls daily from whistleblowers asking for updates on the status of their claims. Several times per month, the Whistleblower Office also responds to members of Congress asking for status updates on behalf of whistleblowers who are their constituents. The Whistleblower Office responds to these requests only by stating if a claim is open or closed. Responding to these types of requests diverts Whistleblower Office resources from processing claims.

During the Whistleblower Office and SME initial reviews and examination, IRS has little contact with whistleblowers. Operating divisions may offer debrief meetings to whistleblowers to clarify information about their submissions, but these meetings may be the only interaction between IRS and whistleblowers until IRS rejects a claim or decides to issue an award. Examiners do not actively involve whistleblowers in their work because they need to build their case independent of the whistleblower's involvement to be able to corroborate the information provided and to ensure they do not receive tainted information.

There are some statutory exceptions to section 6103 that allow IRS to disclose tax information when it is necessary in conducting investigations and gathering information to administer the tax code. Under section 6103(k)(6), IRS may disclose taxpayer return information to a whistleblower to the extent necessary for investigative purposes.[23] Another exception, section 6103(n), allows IRS to enter into contracts with outside parties for services for purposes of tax administration. IRS could enter into a section 6103(n) contract with whistleblowers for analytic services and could disclose tax information necessary to obtain those services.[24] Whistleblowers who enter into section 6103(n) contracts must comply with IRS's safeguards of tax information and are subject to statutory civil and criminal penalties for unauthorized disclosure, which include fines and jail time. If IRS discloses tax information to whistleblowers under section 6103(k)(6), whistleblowers would not be subject to penalties for unauthorized disclosure.

The decision to enter into section 6103(n) contracts rests with the operating divisions; it is not directed by Chief Counsel or the Whistleblower Office, although they may provide advice to the operating divisions. Section 6103(n) contracts are intended to be used rarely by IRS in processing whistleblower claims,[25] and as of April 28, 2011, IRS had not entered into any contracts with whistleblowers. Operating division officials stated they have not yet had a claim that necessitated this increased level of interaction with a whistleblower to gather information about the taxpayer.

According to operating division, Chief Counsel, and Whistleblower Office officials, IRS does not have specific criteria for when a section 6103(n) contract should be offered to a whistleblower, other than it should be used rarely. According to IRS officials, each claim needs to be examined based on its facts and circumstances and generally IRS has the authority and tools to collect any information that a whistleblower could bring forward. Although no section 6103(n) contracts have been offered, IRS officials told us that one situation where a section 6103(n) contract would be useful is if, in the course of an examination, a taxpayer provided documents or testimony to IRS that contradicted information a whistleblower provided. IRS agents could use a section 6103(n) contract to share some tax information with the whistleblower in investigating the inconsistency.

Also, rejection letters IRS sends to whistleblowers do not state why IRS denied a request for an award. IRS officials told us that to provide the reason would violate section 6103. For example, the Whistleblower Office may reject a claim because an examination did not result in an additional tax assessment, but sharing this fact with the whistleblower discloses that IRS conducted an examination. Whistleblowers whose claims for awards are denied can challenge IRS's decision in U.S. Tax Court, although it is uncertain if they will learn the reason for the claim rejection during the appeal process.[26] According to Whistleblower Office officials, whistleblowers have appealed more than 20 award denials under the expanded whistleblower program and they expect the frequency of these appeals to increase.

According to whistleblower attorneys we interviewed, whistleblowers can be frustrated by the lack of communication from IRS regarding their claims. Because some whistleblowers risk their careers by filing a claim, they want to know that IRS is maximizing the information they provide. The attorneys said that IRS not interacting with the whistleblower for long periods of time and not using whistleblowers as resources during investigations discourages whistleblowers and may deter some from coming forward with claims, although we could not verify the latter point.

The Director of the Whistleblower Office told us that many of the steps IRS takes in the whistleblower process, including limiting interaction with the whistleblower, are aimed at protecting all interested parties—the privacy of the taxpayer's information, the identity of the whistleblower, and the integrity of the IRS examination. For example, IRS examiners need to build cases independent of whistleblowers and corroborate all of the information whistleblowers provide. This independent process ensures that examinations are not overly influenced by whistleblowers who have a financial stake in the outcome of examinations; that the identity of a whistleblower is not disclosed; and that taxpayers receive fair and defensible examinations.

One mechanism through which the Whistleblower Office communicates program progress and outcomes to the whistleblower community is the Whistleblower Office's annual report to Congress, which outlines the program's operations for a given fiscal year. This report, which is required by the act that established the Whistleblower Office, is to include an analysis of the program's operations and outcomes and any legislative or administrative recommendations on how to improve the program. The act does not specify what data IRS should include in the report. The reports issued to date contain limited data on claims submitted to the expanded whistleblower program. For example, the 2010 annual report, the most recent report available, included the number of whistleblowers and the number of taxpayers identified, but did not provide data on the time taken for claims to move through the process or specific information on rejected claims. The lack of such data limits Congress's ability to effectively oversee the program. Reporting such additional data could also improve the transparency of the program, which may result in additional whistleblowers coming forward.

Some Whistleblower Attorneys Said Award Payment Issues May Discourage Whistleblowers

As IRS begins paying awards under the expanded whistleblower program, some in the whistleblower community are frustrated by some issues that they see as unfair to whistleblowers. For example, according to whistleblower attorneys we spoke with, net operating loss (NOL) carryforwards remain an issue with the whistleblower program because they are excluded from the definition of collected proceeds.[27]

If a whistleblower's information results in a reduction in NOL, IRS may not realize a financial benefit for years until the company has a positive tax liability.

If the NOL is not exhausted within 10 years or the taxpayer goes bankrupt, IRS may never realize a financial benefit. When whistleblowers bring information to the IRS, they may not know the NOL position of the taxpayer on whom they are blowing the whistle. According to whistleblower attorneys, denying an award because a targeted taxpayer has a NOL carryover is inherently unfair if IRS eventually receives a financial benefit when the NOLs are exhausted.

Some of the attorneys noted that this issue may discourage whistleblowers from coming forward because it adds additional uncertainty to the process and may make submitting a claim not worth the risks to their careers. IRS officials told us that they plan to develop further guidance on collected proceeds and NOLs.

Furthermore, according to the attorneys, IRS's 28 percent tax withholding policy on expanded whistleblower program award payments could result in IRS overwithholding taxes for some whistleblowers, especially those who are represented by attorneys. Attorney fees, which may be 30 percent or more of the total award, are deductible from gross income and reduce the taxable amount of an award.

IRS previously did not withhold taxes on payments made under the original whistleblower program, where awards have been capped at $10 million, but it has recently begun withholding on any awards totaling over $10,000. Overwithheld funds can be refunded when the whistleblower files a tax return for the tax year of the award, but there could be a year or more between award payment and the refund of the overwithheld portion of the award.

IRS does not have a process in place to negotiate an adjusted withholding rate with whistleblowers based on their individual circumstances because the ability to deduct attorney fees is dependent on whistleblowers paying their attorney after receiving awards, which may not always happen. Whistleblower Office officials told us they would rather have a single rate that applies to all whistleblowers paid more than $10,000 than become involved in the independent relationship between whistleblowers and their attorneys.

Other Agencies and Whistleblower Attorneys Identified Options That Could Potentially Improve IRS's Whistleblower Program but Involve Trade-Offs

Federal and state whistleblower programs we reviewed have features with potential benefits that could improve IRS's expanded whistleblower program. Whistleblower attorneys we interviewed also suggested changes they thought could improve the program. Based on these program reviews and interviews, we compiled options that could apply to IRS's whistleblower program, analyzed their potential advantages and disadvantages, and identified strategies that could mitigate the disadvantages.[28] These options, along with the advantages, disadvantages, and mitigation strategies, are presented in table 5, approximately in order of their place in the whistleblower claim review process.

Table 5. Options to Enhance IRS's Whistleblower Program, Their Potential Advantages and Disadvantages, and Potential Strategies for Mitigating Disadvantages

Option and programs utilizing the option	Potential advantages	Potential disadvantages	Potential strategies for mitigating disadvantages
Increase initial vetting • Texas Informant's Recovery Program conducts significant initial research, leading to investigation of a small percentage of claims	• Could weed out claims that are likely to be rejected later in the process, increasing the likelihood that examinations yield revenue	• Resource constraints limit the Whistleblower Office's ability to increase vetting • Benefit of reviewing claims earlier in the process is uncertain	• Developing criteria for claims more likely to generate awards could expedite claim processing
Implement time targets for SME review process • Texas Informant's Recovery Program asks for the audit to be complete—or provide a reason why it is not complete—within 6 months	• Could help ensure that claims are completed in a timely fashion • Could aid in ensuring that the statute of limitation does not expire	• Time targets often are recommendations with no consequences for not meeting them • Needed review time may vary widely based on the facts and	• An action—such as approval or a check-in bythe Whistleblower Office—could be required if the time targetis eclipsed

Option and programs utilizing the option	Potential advantages	Potential disadvantages	Potential strategies for mitigating disadvantages
The Department of Justice has 60 days to accept or decline False Claims Act claims, with options for extension with court approval		• circumstances of each claim Time targets could create negative incentives to rush the processing of a claim and not be as thorough with it	
Implement "checkpoints" for the Whistleblower Office to monitor claims that have eclipsed a recommended time target • No other programs	• Could help ensure that claims are completed in a timely fashion • Could aid in ensuring that the statute of limitation does not expire • Allows for flexibility in length of time a claim takes to process	• Because the Whistleblower Office would only be inquiring on the status of a claim, would not necessarily lead to quicker processing	• After the check-in, agreed upon actions between operating divisions and the Whistleblower Office could prompt action on a claim
Regularly communicate claim progress to whistleblower • Commodity Futures Trading Commission plans to regularly update whistleblowers on their claim status	• Could reduce information solicitations from whistleblowers, freeing up Whistleblower Office resources • Might provide a method of holding IRS accountable	• Tax information may be improperly disclosed • Benefit may be limited if whistleblowers do not change behavior with additional information • Section 6103(n) contracts would not allow for sharing of claim status because it does not show a benefit to tax administration	• Amend section 6103 to allow for sharing of claim progress information withwhistleblowers with sanctions for redisclosure

Table 5. (Continued).

Increase interaction with whistleblowers during investigation process Securities and Exchange Commission intends to interact with whistleblowers	• Whistleblowers' intimate knowledge of the information they provide and the targeted taxpayers could help IRS conduct examinations	• Tax information may be improperly disclosed	• IRS could utilize a section 6103(n) contract to help prevent redisclosure of tax information and impose strict penalties for doing so
Communicate reason for claim rejection to whistleblowers • Centers for Medicare and Medicaid Services' Incentive Rewards Program provides information to informants on the reason their claim was rejected	• Could cut down on whistleblowers appealing rejections in court	• Tax information may be improperly disclosed if additional information is shared • Section 6103(n) contracts would not allow for sharing of claim rejection reasons because it does not show a benefit to tax administration	• Providing aggregate information to Congress and the public in the annual report could provide common reasonsclaims are rejected • Section 6103 could be amended to allow IRS to communicate rejection reasons to whistleblowers with sanctions for redisclosure
Add a qui tam provision to allow whistleblowers to pursue claims independently • Department of Justice / False Claims Act • New York Attorney General's Bureau of Taxpayer Protection – False Claims Act	• Could provide accountability for IRS to make timely decisions on whether to pursue claims • Could leverage resources of outside counsel in processing whistleblower claims	• Could increase the risk of abuse of the whistleblower program, as individuals could pursue meritless claims • Claims filed in court are part of the public record, which could result in the disclosure of tax information • Qui tam tax claims would likely target specific acts whereas IRS examines a taxpayer's entire	• As with some False Claims Act claims, tax claims could be filed "under seal" of the court to avoid disclosure • Requiring a high dollar threshold for underpayment could reduce the number of meritless claims

Option and programs utilizing the option	Potential advantages	Potential disadvantages	Potential strategies for mitigating disadvantages
Public communication of awards decisions • Department of Justice / False Claims Act	• Could generate increased public awareness of the program, potentially leading to increased claims	• Could result in public disclosure of tax information and notify the taxpayer of the existence of a whistleblower	• Decisions could be announced in aggregate without using tax information, such as in the annual report to Congress

Source: GAO analysis.

While there are potential advantages to all identified options, it is difficult to determine if the advantages outweigh the disadvantages for many options. For options that could involve the disclosure of tax information, Treasury guidance states that any proposed exception to section 6103 must demonstrate substantial benefits.[29] Whether informing whistleblowers about why their claims were rejected would produce benefits, such as fewer appeals, is unclear. The Director of the Whistleblower Office did not see net benefits from developing criteria on when section 6103(n) contracts would be appropriate or desirable, due to the varying facts and circumstances of whistleblower claims.

Likewise, it is unclear whether greater Whistleblower Office claim vetting would improve the efficiency of investigations and what additional resources might be needed. Adding a qui tam provision—which allows autonomy for whistleblowers and their counsel to pursue claims independently in court after the agency chooses not to pursue—could encourage IRS to make more timely decisions on whether to pursue a claim. However, a qui tam provision would alter the tax examination process in uncertain ways. Because the suit would likely be focused on the issue identified by the whistleblower, IRS officials said a qui tam provision might favor maximizing the whistleblowers award rather than identifying the correct tax liability.

CONCLUSION

The goal of the expanded whistleblower program is to encourage whistleblowers to come forward with information on substantial tax underreporting that, collectively, could help IRS reduce the tax gap and encourage greater voluntary compliance. For the program to be successful, whistleblowers need to have confidence in the program's processes and outcomes. IRS's claim review process is designed to ensure the integrity of the program, and the many steps involved can take years to complete. Some of the steps in the process are necessarily outside the Whistleblower Office's control in order to, for example, protect the independence of examinations and avoid superseding other enforcement priorities.

However, without more complete data about claim processing time and outcomes, IRS has limited information about the efficiency of the program. Such data could help IRS management assess the efficiency of current processes and evaluate potential improvements. In addition to collecting more complete data, establishing time targets for all operating division initial reviews and following up on claims that exceed these targets could serve to indicate the priority whistleblower claims should receive, set expectations for the length of time they should generally take to review, and focus attention on claims exceeding time targets.

Other steps could improve whistleblower submissions and reporting to Congress. Collecting additional information on Form 211 could aid IRS in evaluating whistleblowers' credibility and perhaps speed up the claim review process. Including more information in the annual Whistleblower Office report to Congress could enhance Congress's ability to oversee the program and increase public confidence in the program, which could encourage more whistleblowers to submit claims.

RECOMMENDATIONS FOR EXECUTIVE ACTION

To improve the effectiveness of IRS's expanded whistleblower program, we recommend the Commissioner of Internal Revenue direct the Whistleblower Office Director to take the following seven actions:

- record time-in-step information for all claims by identified taxpayer in E-TRAK;
- adjust E-TRAK's tracking feature to more accurately count the number of days claims remain in each step;
- track the reasons for claim rejections by broad categories;
- track the reasons claims are listed as suspended by broad categories;

- establish a process by which the Whistleblower Office routinely follows up on claims that have been in the operating division SME initial review step more than a targeted number of days;
- redesign Form 211 to include stand-alone questions on the following information:
- the relationship of the whistleblower to the target taxpayer,
- the employer of the whistleblower,
- whether the whistleblower has submitted the information to any other federal or state agencies, and
- whether the whistleblower has included all information relevant to the claim; and
- provide additional summary statistics in future annual reports to Congress, including data on the length of time claims remain at each step of the review process, data on the length of time from claim receipt to payments, reasons for claim rejections, aggregate information on awards paid, and total amount of whistleblower payments.

Further, we recommend that the Commissioner of Internal Revenue direct the Commissioners of LB&I and TE/GE to develop targets for how long SME reviews should take before being flagged for follow-up.

AGENCY COMMENTS AND OUR EVALUATION

We provided a draft of this report to the Commissioner of Internal Revenue and offered other agencies we spoke with the opportunity to comment on the draft. IRS and SEC provided technical comments, which we incorporated into the report as appropriate. We received written comments from IRS's Deputy Commissioner for Services and Enforcement.

The Deputy Commissioner stated that IRS generally agreed with our recommendations, and said it would incorporate the recommendations as IRS continues to make improvements to the operating processes and procedures of the whistleblower program. The Deputy Commissioner noted, however, that resource availability could affect the implementation of recommended improvements. He stated that recommended modifications to E-TRAK to more accurately reflect program information will be considered as part of an overall evaluation of E-TRAK adjustments and enhancements, which will begin in the near future, and that IRS would make the appropriate improvements as feasible given resource constraints and competing priorities. Also, the Deputy Commissioner agreed to consider whether time targets for operating divisions are appropriate as part of IRS's efforts to ensure that subject matter experts' initial review of whistleblower cases is completed in a timely manner. IRS will consider including additional summary statistical information in its annual report to Congress, but did not specify what information.

We acknowledge that resources must be considered when considering improvements to the whistleblower program, but IRS risks not being able to maximize the program's effectiveness without implementing the recommendations in this report. Collecting more data on review timeliness and outcomes and establishing time targets could help IRS to make more effective decisions on allocating its resources and aid its ongoing program assessment. Congress has expressed concern about the limited data available about the whistleblower program and including more information and data in the Whistleblower Office annual report could improve oversight of, and increase confidence in, the program.

James R. White
Director, Tax Issues
Strategic Issues Team

APPENDIX I: SCOPE AND METHODOLOGY

To assess how the Internal Revenue Service (IRS) manages the expanded whistleblower program, including communicating within IRS, we reviewed the Tax Relief and Health Care Act of 2006, which required that IRS establish the Whistleblower Office and administer the expanded award program; reviewed IRS documents on the whistleblower program, including Internal Revenue Manual section 25.2.2, which outlines roles and responsibilities in the expanded whistleblower program; and reviewed GAO's body of work on internal control standards. We also interviewed staff from the IRS Whistleblower Office, representatives from the three business operating divisions—Small Business/Self Employed, Large Business and International, and Tax Exempt and Government Entities— that handle whistleblower claims, and representatives from other IRS divisions—Chief Counsel and Criminal Investigations—that are part of the whistleblower process. We also spoke with nine attorneys who represent tax whistleblowers to determine the concerns of whistleblowers regarding the length of time the whistleblower claim review process takes. Seven of these attorneys were a nongeneralizable sample of attorneys recommended by IRS as frequent representatives of whistleblowers submitting claims to the whistleblower program. Whistleblower attorneys have a clear financial interest in the outcome of whistleblower claims. However, interviewing them allowed us to obtain broad viewpoints of the IRS whistleblower program while keeping whistleblowers' identities confidential. To report statistics on whistleblower claims, we analyzed data from the Whistleblower Office's E-TRAK system. We found that the data generated from E-TRAK on claim status was sufficiently reliable for the purposes of our report.

To evaluate how IRS communicates with whistleblowers and the public, we reviewed Internal Revenue Code section 6103, which governs the protection of tax information. We interviewed staff from the IRS Whistleblower Office and the operating divisions and other offices that are part of the whistleblower process. We interviewed the attorneys for their opinions on how IRS communication procedures affect whistleblowers and the processing of whistleblower claims. We also spoke with the National Taxpayer Advocate to identify potential privacy concerns for targeted taxpayers.[1]

To determine what lessons, if any, can be learned from IRS's and whistleblowers' past experiences with the Whistleblower Office as well as other governmental efforts that could improve the IRS whistleblower program, we identified federal and state programs that were similar to IRS's whistleblower program. At the federal level, we interviewed officials from programs that provide financial awards for bringing information to the government on specific issues that result in awards paid to whistleblowers. Specifically, we interviewed officials from the Department of Justice, which administers claims made under the False Claims Act; the Incentive Rewards Program at the Centers for Medicare and Medicaid Services; and the new whistleblower programs established under the Dodd-Frank Wall Street Reform and Consumer Protection Act at the Securities and Exchange Commission and the Commodity Futures Trading Commission. We identified states with tax whistleblower reward programs—New York, Florida, and Texas[2]—and interviewed representatives from these programs and reviewed relevant program documents. To identify potential lessons learned from IRS's past experiences, we spoke with IRS officials and attorneys who represent tax whistleblowers and reviewed academic literature on tax whistleblowers. From these interviews and document and literature reviews, we created a list of options and asked IRS and whistleblower attorneys on their thoughts of the advantages and disadvantages of these options in the context of the IRS whistleblower program.

We conducted this performance audit from September 2010 to August 2011 in accordance with generally accepted government auditing standards. Those standards require that we plan and perform the audit to obtain sufficient, appropriate evidence to provide a reasonable basis for our findings and conclusions based on our audit objectives. We believe that the evidence obtained provides a reasonable basis for our findings and conclusions based on our audit objectives.

End Notes

1 Pub. L. No. 109-432, div. A, title IV, § 406, 120 Stat. 2922 (Dec. 20, 2006).

2 IRS estimated that it would eventually collect about $55 billion of the gross tax gap through late payments and IRS enforcement actions, leaving a net tax gap of around $290 billion.

3 Section 6103 of the Internal Revenue Code governs the protection of taxpayer returns and return information. IRS's view is that reporting the exact number of awards before a sufficient number of payments have been made would violate section 6103, which prohibits disclosing tax information either directly or indirectly. IRS has not yet paid a sufficient number of awards to meet the threshold for aggregate public disclosure. We deferred to IRS's interpretation of the disclosure rules and have not reported the exact number of awards paid.

4 See An Act to Amend Existing Laws Relating to Internal Revenue, and for other Purposes, ch. 169, § 7, 14 Stat. 471, 473 (1867).

5 Taxpayer Bill of Rights 2, Pub. L. No. 104-168, title XII, § 1209, 110 Stat. 1452 (July 30, 1996).

6 See 26 U.S.C. § 7623. For the purposes of our report, we refer to the rules laid out in Internal Revenue Code section 7623(a) as the original program and 7623(b) as the expanded program.

7 The Small Business/Self-Employed (SB/SE) division investigates claims against small businesses with assets of less than $10 million and self-employed taxpayers. The Large Business and International (LB&I) division investigates claims against corporations and partnerships with assets of $10 million or more. The Tax Exempt and Government Entities (TE/GE) division investigates claims against pension plans, exempt organizations, and government entities. Another operating division, Wage and Investment (W&I), is responsible for individual taxpayers without business income. Due to the high income and tax criteria for the expanded whistleblower program, W&I is not involved in investigating whistleblower claims under the expanded program.

8 CI has investigative jurisdiction over tax, money laundering, and Bank Secrecy Act violations. It is a principal office and not an operating division under IRS's organizational structure. However, for the purposes of our report, we use the term operating division to refer to LB&I, SB/SE, TE/GE, and CI, the divisions that process whistleblower claims.

9 Internal Revenue Manual 25.2.2.1 (06/18/2010).

[10] Rewards and Awards for Information Relating to Violations of Internal Revenue Laws, 76 Fed. Reg. 2852 (Jan. 18, 2011).

[11] Nonresident aliens who receive whistleblower awards may be subject to different withholding rates.

[12] Both of these whistleblower programs were mandated in the Dodd-Frank Wall Street Reform and Consumer Protection Act, Pub. L. No. 111-203, 124 Stat. 1376 (Jul. 21, 2010).

[13] As of April 25, 2011, of the claims currently assigned to the operating divisions, 16.7 percent were assigned to CI, 32.6 percent to LB&I, 48 percent to SB/SE and 2.7 percent to TE/GE.

[14] Among all examinations, including examinations of whistleblower claims, the average cycle time—the time from the start of an examination to its completion—is 211 days in SB/SE and 322 days in LB&I.

[15] 26 U.S.C. § 6511(a). For example, a taxpayer's deduction may be denied because the taxpayer could not produce supporting documentation during an examination. If, within 2 years of paying the tax, the taxpayer obtains supporting documentation, the taxpayer may apply for a refund for the associated documented deduction.

[16] If a submission in total would be greater than the $2 million threshold for the expanded program but each taxpayer claim within the submission does not meet the threshold, paying on the taxpayer claims individually would negatively impact the whistleblower's appeal rights, which differ under the original and expanded programs.

[17] In August, 2009, the Treasury Inspector General for Tax Administration (TIGTA) reported that as of March 2009, E-TRAK could not provide management information reports and that not all key data was successfully transferred from the previous tracking systems into E-TRAK. TIGTA made recommendations on how the Whistleblower Office could improve claims data management and IRS agreed with these recommendations. See TIGTA 2009-30-114, Deficiencies Exist in the Control and Timely Resolution of Whistleblower Claims, Aug 20, 2009.

[18] In general, IRS has 3 years from the date a taxpayer files a tax return—not the date a whistleblower submits a claim—to complete an examination and assess the taxes owed unless the taxpayer agrees to an extension or under specific exceptions that allow IRS to extend the statute unilaterally, such as for cases of fraud.

[19] The Whistleblower Office does not actively manage or track claims that are approaching their statute of limitations, although once identified in the Whistleblower Office initial review process, analysts, SMEs, and other IRS officials consider the statute of limitations when prioritizing their work load. Additionally, according to Whistleblower Office officials, examiners face performance consequences if they do not complete an assigned examination before the statute of limitations expires. Nevertheless, IRS officials acknowledge that some claims are ultimately rejected because the statute of limitations has expired; however, they told us that this most frequently happens because the statute has already expired or is close to expiring by the time a whistleblower submits a claim.

[20] E-TRAK has added new step fields before. In 2010, IRS added the "suspended case" step, which, according to the analyst who completed this addition, required less than an hour to complete because it involved adding one additional choice to an existing list of step choices. To reconfigure E-TRAK to accommodate a new field, the analyst estimated it may take days or weeks of direct programming time followed by additional time to schedule the changes to become functional.

[21] See GAO, Internal Control Standards: Internal Control Management and Evaluation Tool, GAO-01-1008G (Washington, D.C.: Aug. 2001).

[22] Section 6103 of the Internal Revenue Code governs the protection of taxpayer returns and return information. Under section 6103(b)(1), a return means any tax or information return, declaration of estimated tax, or claim for refund filed with IRS. Return information means a taxpayer's identity, the nature, source, or amount of income, payments, receipts, deductions, exemptions, credits, assets, liabilities, net worth, tax liability, tax withheld, deficiencies, overassessments, or tax payments, whether the taxpayer's return was, is being, or will be examined or subject to investigation, or any other data received by, recorded by, prepared by, furnished to, or collected by the IRS. 26 U.S.C. § 6103(b)(2).

[23] 26 C.F.R. § 301.6103(k)(6)-1.

[24] 26 C.F.R. § 301.6103(n)-2. The Internal Revenue Manual advises IRS employees to use section 6103(n) contracts to obtain the services of experts for investigative purposes rather than section 6103(k)(6) whenever possible. IRM 11.3.21.4 (03-28-2008).

[25] In the Joint Committee on Taxation's (JCT) Technical Explanation of the expanded whistleblower program, JCT noted that IRS could enter into section 6103(n) tax administration contracts when whistleblower assistance is necessary to analyze information provided or investigate the matter claimed. JCT also noted that IRS's use of section 6103(n) contracts should be infrequent and only when the review of the claim could not be properly or timely completed without disclosing taxpayer's return information. JCX-50-06.

[26] The Tax Court has jurisdiction to review IRS's whistleblower award determinations under the expanded program, including the denial of an award claim. See Cooper v. Commissioner, 135 T.C. 70 (July 8, 2010). However, the Tax Court's jurisdiction does not extend to reviewing IRS's decision of whether to pursue administrative or judicial action against the taxpayer. If IRS denies an award because no tax, interest, or penalty was collected from the taxpayer based on the whistleblower's information, that decision will not be reviewed by the Tax Court. Cooper v. Commissioner, 136 T.C. 30 (June, 20, 2011). As of June 21, 2011, the Tax Court had not published a case discussing the merits of IRS's whistleblower award determination where amounts were collected from the taxpayer.

[27] A net operating loss occurs when, in a tax year, a company's deductible losses are greater than its tax liability, resulting in no taxable income. NOLs that exceed taxable income can be carried back generally for 2 tax years or carried forward for 10 or more years. A company may not realize the NOL credit if it does not have taxable income before the NOL expires.

[28] For a more detailed discussion of our methodology, see app. I.

[29] Department of the Treasury, Office of Tax Policy, Report to The Congress on the Scope and Use of Taxpayer Confidentiality and Disclosure Provisions, Volume I (Washington, D.C., 2000).

End Notes for Appendix I

[1] The National Taxpayer Advocate heads the Taxpayer Advocate Service, an independent organization within IRS which provides services to taxpayers seeking help in resolving problems with IRS.

[2] Oregon also has a whistleblower rewards statute, but the program is inactive.

INDEX

L

M

N

O

P

Q

R

S